Daughters

of

Another

Path

DAUGHTERS OF ANOTHER PATH

Experiences of American Women Choosing Islam

by

Carol L. Anway

Yawna Publications
P.O. Box 27
Lee's Summit, MO 64063
Yawna@iland.net

First Printing December 1995   Fifth Printing August 2001
Second Printing May 1996   Sixth Printing November 2002
Third Printing October, 1998
Fourth Printing May, 2000

ISBN: 0-9647169-0-9

Library of Congress Catalog Card Number: 95-90490

Publisher's Cataloging in Publication
(Prepared by Quality Books Inc.)

Anway, Carol Anderson.
   Daughters of another path: experiences of American women choosing Islam / Carol L. Anway.
   p. cm.
   Includes bibliographical references and index.
   ISBN 0-9647169-0-9

   1. Muslim converts—United States. 2. Women, Muslim—United States. 3. Conversion. I. Title

BP170.5.A1A69 1995   291.4'2
**   QBI95-20259**

ACKNOWLEDGMENT

My deep appreciation is extended first of all to my daughter, Jodi Anway Mohammadzadeh, who has caused me to stretch and view the world through another window. Our whole family has been enriched and enlarged by our venture with her to see life with new perspective and insights. Her contribution throughout the project and writing of the book has been so helpful—the editorial reviews, the rewriting, the title, the feedback.

My initial encouragement and zeal for the project was sparked by Dr. Jamilah Kolocotronis Jitmoud and Susan Elsayyad, both American-born women who became Muslims and are currently teachers at the Kansas City Islamic School. They met with Jodi and me and helped us define the project, expressing a need in their lives for such a reconciling resource.

I would love to personally meet each of the 53 women who shared their conversion stories by responding to the questionnaires. Each one was an inspiration and testimony to what she has chosen—to be a Muslim woman, submissive to the will of God.

Working with my editor and long-time friend, Talitha Pennington, has been a joy. She required so much of me as she helped me present this book to you in a concise, well-organized form. I needed her!

And thanks to Joe, my husband and the love of my life, for support and encouragement through this and all our years together.

Table of Contents

Introduction 1

1. **Daughters of Another Path**:
   Women Becoming Muslim in America 3

2. **The Beginning Path**:
   Growing Up Christian in an American Family 9

3. **Changing Paths**:
   American Women Choosing to Become Muslim 19

4. **Forsaking the Previous Path**:
   Reactions of Relatives 43

5. **Journeying the Muslim Path**:
   Living and Practicing Islamic Principles 63

6. **Accepting the Daughter's Journey**:
   Reconciling Lifestyle Choices Between Daughter
   and Parents 93

7. **Following the Path into Marriage**:
   When Two Become One in Islam 111

8. **Raising Children in Another Path**:
   Muslim Children in American Society 129

9. **Respecting Divergent Paths**:
   Working Together to Build and
   Maintain Relationships 145

10. **The Daughters Speak Out**:
   What Muslim Converts Would Like Us to Know ... 159

Epilogue 173

Appendix A: Letter and Questionnaire: American-Born
Women Converted to Islam 177

Appendix B: Questionnaire: Parents of American-Born
Women Converted to Islam 183

Appendix C: One Woman's Story in Response to the
Questionnaire 185

Glossary of Islamic terms 197

Bibliography Reference Materials for
Understanding Islam 201

Index 209

DEDICATION

The world is constantly growing and changing. All persons have a road to travel and a path to find to bring meaning to their lives. Even though in the United States and Canada we may be bombarded with information on how others in the world live their lives, we somehow don't catch on. We are prone to segregate ourselves in our own economic, religious, or ethnic groups and resist bumping into other cultures and ideas. We tend to be shaped by the headlines and daily news reporting, which can feed our fears and reinforce stereotypes that are often misleading.

This book is written in dedication to you, the reader, because you have taken the time to look beyond what you know. You have sought to find out about American-born women who have chosen the path of Islam. One of these Muslim women may be your classmate, your co–worker, your grocer, your neighbor, your cousin, your niece, your grandchild, and yes, maybe even your daughter.

Introduction

The first time I saw *Fiddler on the Roof* I became upset with Tevye, the father who was so tied to his traditions that he broke the ties with one daughter and almost with the other two because they chose different "traditions." *Those girls are good persons who will live good lives even if it isn't in the tradition of their parents. Why not leave them alone?* I thought. Then I learned firsthand about the struggle that goes with having one's child break with traditional expectations. Like Tevye, I experienced rejection and anger and grief.

Our daughter, Jodi, seemed to learn well one of the concepts I wanted to teach her: "Missouri is not the only place in the world; there is a whole world out there to explore. God loves all people, so we need to be open to them and have a global concept of life." I was happy that some of her friends were from other countries.

Then I began to see that she was getting serious about Reza, a young man from Iran. Soon she announced her intention to marry him and eventually live in Iran. He was a person that we really enjoyed knowing. But to have our daughter marry him and go off to a foreign country. . . . I replayed in my mind the scene of Tevye watching his second daughter board the train, knowing he would probably never see her again.

In time, however, my husband, Joe, and I came to accept the idea and knew that we had grown as a result. Although Muslim, Reza seemed open and accepting, and we felt that Jodi was secure in her beliefs in Christ and our church. Her marriage in the church at Warrensburg was a tremendously happy occasion. Since Reza and Jodi were completing their degrees, I told myself it would be years before they would go to Iran. Perhaps by then they would change their minds.

Within two years my fears about her move to Iran were superseded by a greater one—Jodi's decision to convert to Islam. It had never occurred to me that she might voluntarily choose a different religious tradition than that of our family. But she did. This book presents my story, and Jodi's, and the changes that occurred in our relationship with her commitment to become Muslim.

Also presented are the stories of several other American-born women who have converted to Islam—their backgrounds, their reasons for converting, their acceptance of the principles of Islam which they find so appealing, and what it has meant for their lives and their families. Leaving behind the Western modernistic society that shaped them, they have committed themselves to a way of life dictated by Islamic principles as interpreted in the community of Muslims with whom they worship and with whom they associate.

My hope is that the reader of this book will gain a clearer understanding of the young, American-born women who have chosen Islam, how and why they converted, and the strength that choosing this path has given to them. As these women describe living out Islamic principles in their daily lives, non-Muslims can not only learn about the Islamic way but also discover how best to relate to these Muslim women in the workplace, as relatives and as friends or acquaintances.

For many of us, these are our daughters, sisters, granddaughters, cousins, friends, or co-workers who have chosen another path of faith to God. May this book be an opportunity to cross over for a brief time to understand their approach and commitment to another path.

1. Daughters of Another Path
Women Becoming Muslim In America

She may be shopping at the mall, driving or riding in a car, studying in university classes, or sharing an office in the workplace. Her dress is modest, a scarf covering her hair with only her face and hands uncovered (although even her face may be veiled). She wears outfits that are usually neat but not showy, sometimes reflecting foreign fashion. She is very conspicuous in our society, often triggering thoughts like "strange religion," "terrorist," "fundamentalist," "mystery," "foreign," or "oil," and she makes us feel uncomfortable and alienated.

Expecting to hear a heavy accent when speaking to her, one may be shocked if she sounds just like any American—hummmm!

"Where are you from?" the curious observer might ask. "Toledo, Ohio," she may reply. But it could have been any other city or town.

"Oh, really?" the observer responds, somewhat taken back realizing that she is one of us.

A growing number of American-born women in the United States and Canada have converted to Islam and call themselves Muslim like any other follower of Islam. Many hold to the tradition of wearing hijab* (covering) in public. Others don't feel it necessary to cover and are, therefore, less noticeable but are

---

*A Glossary of Islamic Terms, following Appendix C, gives definitions for all Islamic terms referred to in the text or quotes.

also among the growing number of converts in the United States and Canada.

No one knows for sure how many of the world's one billion Muslims live in the United States and Canada, but the American Muslim Council of Washington, D.C., estimates the Muslim population to be between 6 and 8 million including American-born converts, those who have immigrated, and a growing number of children born Muslim in America. Thus Islam may already have more followers in the United States than Judaism which has 5.5 million adherents. This would make Islam the second-leading religion after Christianity. The growing number of mosques and student centers also reflects the emerging presence of Islam. Around 1985 there were approximately six hundred mosques, student centers, and other Islamic centers with the numbers growing.

Muslim history in the United States is fairly short. The booklet, *A Century of Islam in America*,[1] indicates three waves of Muslim immigration. The first occurred in 1875 with migrant laborers, uneducated and unskilled workers willing to work hard. Many stayed, but those who returned home encouraged others to come to America. The second wave in the 1930s was stopped by World War II. The third wave of immigrants in the '50s and '60s tended to be well-educated and from influential families, often trying to escape political oppression or to obtain higher education.

Muslims tend to group in the larger cities where they have support from each other. Many of the larger universities have active Muslim groups. It is here they learn from and help each other live the Muslim lifestyle that is at times difficult to blend with the schedule and activities of the American society. Muslims are obligated to follow the practices of Islam in every detail in daily life. These practices are dictated by the Qur'an and the Hadith (the reported sayings, deeds, and practices of Muhammad), and by the other examples attributed to Prophet Muhammad. Unique in many Western settings is the right to practice religion as one desires, which extends to Muslims the opportunity to live their lives Islamically as interpreted in their community.

Western countries once identified as Judeo-Christian countries may need to recognize they are becoming Judeo-Christian-Muslim societies. The growth of Islam in the Western Hemisphere is fast becoming a major topic for media coverage. The expansion of Islam is a major contemporary issue for all North Americans although most Americans know little about either the principles of Islam or its history.

Islam had its beginning in the Arabian Peninsula during the seventh century when Muhammad received divine revelations from God (Allah) through the angel Gabriel. These were received by Muhammad who spoke them orally, and the recitations were eventually written down to form the Qur'an (or Koran), the Muslim's sacred book, which is considered to be the literal and final word of God to the world.

Islam Enters My World

Fourteen years ago our daughter Jodi married a young man from Iran and soon converted to Islam. She began wearing the cover and learning to live and practice as a Muslim. The next few years were a time of grief and adjustment for our family. In the intervening years we have grown to appreciate the strength and commitment of our daughter and her American-Muslim friends.

From this personal experience I decided to collect the stories of American-born women who converted to Islam. I developed and distributed a questionnaire and soon began receiving many personal expressions of strength and faith.

Many North Americans (including United States and Canada) are familiar with the book and movie, *Not Without My Daughter;* the movie, *True Lies;* or other articles and media comments filled with negative portrayals of Muslims. We rarely have the opportunity on a personal level to observe the quality of life that American-born women who have become Muslim have in their

Islamic commitment. I felt that a more positive image was needed, and by gathering and sharing some of the stories of these American-born women who have converted to Islam, that desire within me has been accomplished. The intent is not to use each story in total but to use portions to unfold the stories and faith journeys of some who chose to convert to Islam. Woven in with these stories is my own story as a mother of one who became Muslim. Here is an opportunity to also find out about the beliefs of Islam and how it is lived out on a daily basis by its disciples.

Overview of Survey Results

The questionnaire (Appendix A) was distributed at several Muslim conferences and also mailed to those who heard about the survey and called in, or were referred by others. Of the 350 questionnaires distributed, fifty-three women responded representing diverse regions across North America: Oklahoma, Kansas, Missouri, Virginia, New Jersey, Indiana, Oregon, Alabama, Texas, California, Louisiana, Washington, Illinois, Pennsylvania, Arkansas, Vermont, and Ontario. These fifty-three respondents thoughtfully spent many hours answering the in-depth questions presented to them.

The educational level of the women responding ranges from high school graduate to doctorate. Fifty-three percent hold a bachelor's degree or above. Thirty-five percent of the women have B.A. or B.S. degrees, 12 percent have M.A. or M.S. degrees and 6 percent have M.D. or Ph.D. degrees. At the time they responded, seven of the women were college students working toward a higher degree.

The age range was from twenty-one to forty-seven years of age with 40 percent of the respondents in their twenties, 48 percent in their thirties, and 12 percent in their forties. The number of years the women have been Muslim ranged from six months to twenty-two years. Those who have been Muslim six months to three years constitute 32 percent; four to six years, 24 percent; and seven to ten years, 20 percent. Twenty-four percent of the respondents have been Muslim eleven years or longer with the two longest at nineteen years and twenty-two years.

Approximately 40 percent of the women work outside the home either part-time or full-time, two women have their own in-home businesses, and 12 percent are working toward college degrees. One-half are full-time homemakers with 25 percent of those choosing to home school their children of school age. Although 75 percent of the women have children, not all of the children are of school age. Forty-seven percent send their children to public schools, 11 percent have children enrolled in non-Muslim private schools, 26 percent have children in Islamic schools, and 26 percent home school. This adds up to more than 100 percent because some families have children in two or three of the different school settings.

In observing the common practices of Islam, only two of the women in this survey are not currently wearing hijab full-time. For the most part, all are involved in daily prayers, fasting at Ramadan, and participating in ongoing study regarding Islam. Eighteen percent indicated they eat meats other than halal (approved) meats with the exception of pork which is strictly forbidden.

Ninety percent of the women in the study are married and reflect successful and happy marriages at the time of the survey. They indicate much satisfaction at the position they feel is theirs in the Islamic setting. Some of those who are single as a result of divorce, widowhood, or never marrying indicate that they are uncomfortable at times in Muslim gatherings. They expressed the belief that marriage would give them a better position in the Muslim community. Since being married is considered "the natural state" in the Islamic community, they feel a loss of power, for it is through a husband that they would have connection and input into decisions made at the mosque.

Their responses represent extremely positive reactions to their chosen Muslim lifestyle, by contrast to the more negative stories often heard in the media. As in the American society at large, one can assume the stories of most American-born Muslim women range from happy and well-adjusted, through the in-between "life-is-okay-but" stories, to those stories which contain much grief and unhappiness. In this study, most of the women have found fulfillment and happiness in their decision to live a specific lifestyle—Islam.

Notes

1. Yvonne Y. Haddad, *A Century of Islam* (Washington, D.C.: The Middle East Institute, 1986).

2. The Beginning Path
Growing Up Christian
in an American Family

Jodi dropped out of college during the fall semester of her sophomore year. She was in a state of emotional and spiritual turmoil and moved in with her grandmother because she wasn't sure she could handle living with us.

Later that fall Jodi went with a small group of young adults on a church tour to bring ministry to several congregations and to explore some church historical sites. When she came back from the trip, she told of her experience of emotional healing. "Mom and Dad, I now know what you mean about there being a God—I had an experience with God. As I sat with the group praying, it was like a warm flooding of my soul. It was an assurance that there actually is a God. It was a healing time for me, and now I am ready to start getting on with my life."

But Jodi still was not ready to move back home, so we provided a small apartment in one of our rental houses while she attended the community college where her dad taught.

In that semester, Jodi and Reza became acquainted. An engineering student at the same community college, Reza was a serious young man who held similar moral values that Jodi wanted for her life. Here was someone who could help her be what she really wanted to be.

At Eastertime we were going out of town to visit relatives. We invited Jodi and Reza to go with us. On Easter morning, as we prepared to go to church, Jodi excitedly whispered, "Mom, Reza wants me to marry him and go to Iran to live! Isn't that great?"

No, it wasn't great. Iran was where the hostage crisis was happening. No, this couldn't happen.

All through the Easter service, tears streamed down my face. I kept seeing in my mind the scene from *Fiddler on the Roof* where Tevya sends his second daughter off at the train station, knowing he would never see her again. She sings to her father the song, "Far From the Home I Love." I could not tolerate this!

Reza invited us to his apartment for dinner the next Thursday. Could we come? Well, that would be very nice. Yes, we would like that. It was a pleasant time together—then Reza got to the point. "Joe and Carol, I invited you here because I want to marry Jodi and would like to have your approval."

"When?"

"As soon as possible—by this summer, we hope." He explained their feelings, their friendship, their agreement on values.

We just could not agree. She had college to finish. How would they pay for it? No. No.

But as time went on we could see they were going through with it, approval or not. It was the first of May and I was out of town on a work assignment. As I viewed a video in preparation for the weekend workshop I was to conduct, I watched a segment about a missionary to India. The missionary told about walking miles in rough terrain and hot weather to reach a village. His feet were blistered and sore. When he reached the village, he sat on a tree stump. An old lady of the village came to him with a pan of water, removed his shoes and socks, and bathed his feet. As he looked into her eyes, he said he saw the light of Jesus in those eyes. As I heard the story, I fell on my knees. "God, I have not tried to see anything in Reza. I have only resisted. I will look for your light in his eyes and find acceptance."

When I saw him again after my return, I looked at Reza in a different way. His beautiful dark eyes reflected love, gentleness, and light, and I was overwhelmed with a feeling of acceptance. My husband, Joe, also had come to accept him, so the wedding was planned for the first of August. Reza was a good man. We would share the gospel with him and, perhaps before long, he would become a Christian.

❖ ❖ ❖

How familiar the feelings and emotions are for many of us whose children are young adults. They make choices that we don't agree with. We think we are raising them to take on our values and make the decisions which would fit our lifestyle. But somehow it doesn't work. They have options, and they often choose lifestyles different from the ones we hoped they would choose.

In my collection of stories of American-born women who had converted to Islam, the overwhelming majority described growing up with a religious commitment either because the family required it or because the girl herself wanted to be involved. Only two respondents said religion was not important in their formative years, and one had never been a Christian. Several had dropped out of church because they felt they couldn't get their questions answered, or when they left home, they no longer "had to go" to church because of parental demands. Some of these women were daughters or granddaughters of ministers.

They came from fundamental as well as more liberal denominations. Although 28 percent did not give specific denominations, those mentioned were Catholic, Southern Baptist, Methodist, Christian—Disciples of Christ, Episcopalian, Reorganized Church of Jesus Christ of Latter Day Saints (RLDS), Nazarene Church, Presbyterian, Lutheran, Jehovah's Witness, Quaker, Greek Orthodox, Seventh-Day Adventist, World Wide Church of God, as well as charismatic and born-again Christians. One was a Christian who had become Hindu and another was looking into Judaism. Most came from a religious background and were searching for meaning in their lives during the young adult questioning stage. In the following, some of these women describe their perceptions of the religious environment in their early lives.

Families Who Were Strict in Religious Expectations

Some of the women came from families who were determined that their daughters would be diligent in their church attendance, not only on Sundays but also during the week. The word "strict" was often used to describe the expectations of some families in regard to religion.

❖I was raised as a Catholic. I was taken to church and Sunday school every Sunday because my father insisted and physically forced me and my brothers and sisters to go and told us if we did not go to church we would go to hell. I believed in God and feared him to some extent and asked him for help. When I was seventeen I stopped going to church and had horrible nightmares about the devil coming to get me for about six months or more.

❖My father is a United Methodist minister. My grandfather was a Baptist minister. I was raised in a very religious environment. I went to church almost every day of the week.

❖I grew up a Christian (Seventh-Day Adventist), going to church and to private schools run by the church. I grew up in a strict environment: no non-religious activities from sundown Friday to sundown Saturday, many church activities, restricted diet (not only no pork, but also other things specified in the Bible in the Old Testament), no drinking or smoking, no jewelry, etc. In high school I got disillusioned with the church because I saw so much hypocrisy in it. I stopped going to church and dropped out of high school at seventeen.

These families required what they thought best for their daughters growing up. The women often developed a deep belief in God but going to church became something they had to do, and they were relieved when they were old enough to make their own decisions about church attendance.

Parents Whose Denominational Convictions Were Changing or Weak

Although many parents had deep religious convictions, they had either dropped out of church or were only attending on a part-time basis. Some families were split in regard to denominational allegiance; others changed denominations during the daughter's growing up period. Some of the women expressed dissatisfaction with their religion of origin.

❖When I was a child my family belonged to the World Wide Church of God, but they broke away while I was still young. My father felt that most organized churches were corrupt, but he was (in my opinion) extremely religious. Being raised in this way, I was always seeking some religious fulfillment.

❖I was a born-again Christian—but was not practicing. I didn't go to church because I wasn't interested in the whole overly religious, pressured atmosphere. My mom became a born-again Christian when I was in third grade. We were Catholic before that. I remember Mom having us kneel in front of the TV while she was watching Jim Bakker on TV.

❖My religious commitment was deeply imbedded. My parents did not attend church but sent me with family and friends from the time I was two years old. My parents had and, to some extent, still have moral standards that were taught to me in my youth regardless of their church attendance record. My mother's father is a Pentecostal preacher and my mother had always expressed her ill feelings toward her father for making her go to church three times a week.

❖When I was a child, I went to the Church of God, my father's denomination. Then, when I was a teenager, I went to the Episcopal church with my mom. The reason for the change was because my mom decided to go back to her Episcopal roots. I was not really satisfied with either one.

As reflected by some of the survey respondents, a degree of turmoil or unrest was present in their families in regard to religion. Consequently, the prevailing attitude was one of confusion and doubt.

Women Who Felt a Pull Toward the Religious Experience

Disillusionment, confusion, unanswered questions—these describe the early religious experience of many of the women. However, in spite of frustration, their stories show their devotion, of being in the "search mode" and looking for stability in their religious life.

❖My father is Presbyterian and my mother is Catholic. My father was never active in any church, but Mother tried to raise us Catholic. I was baptized in the Catholic church and received my First Communion at about the age of eight. After that, we only went about once a year. When I was about ten, I became a very active member of a small Presbyterian church nearby. By ninth grade, I was helping the minister's wife teach Sunday school. In high school I started a church youth group by recruiting four of my friends to join me. It was a small group, but we were content to get together to study the Bible, talk about God, and raise money for charities.

These friends and I would sit together and talk about spiritual issues. We debated about questions in our minds: What happens to the people who lived before Jesus came (go to heaven or hell)? Why do some very righteous people automatically go to hell just because they don't believe in Jesus (we thought about Gandhi)? On the other hand, why do some horrible people (like my friend's abusive father) get rewarded with heaven just because they're Christian? Why does a loving and merciful God require a blood sacrifice (Jesus) to forgive people's sins? Why are we guilty of Adam's original sin? Why does the Word of God (Bible) disagree with scientific facts? How can Jesus be God? How can One God be three different things? We debated these things, but never came up with good answers. The church couldn't give us good answers either; they only told us to "have faith."

❖I was raised Catholic, but stopped attending services in high school due to disenchantment on my mother's part. I enjoyed the traditions of the Catholic church and liked the conservative values. There were always many unanswered questions for me even as a child—I could not accept the vague or nonsense answers. I knew even as a small child that these vague areas of faith and philosophy of blind obedience to the clergy were not right.

❖I was a Christian by birth. I had always loved Sunday school and church. In a mixed-up, divorced, dysfunctional family, I was looking for stability, not just from a community but from God. After the age of eighteen I searched from church to church looking for "the answer" only to find more confusing messages from each minister and pastor. I remember always telling my best friend that I wished I could find a church. I always had an empty space inside of me. She would empathize with me and try to encourage me to go on Sundays. But by the age of twenty-two, I had given up on "man-made religion" but not on God.

♣I was raised as a Catholic. My mother practices her faith but my father is not attending mass regularly. Since I was in elementary school, I questioned the teachers (nuns) and parents about the Trinity (who should I pray to: Jesus, God the Father, Holy Spirit? How about the Saints?). I was told there was no explanation and I just had to accept it the way it is. It was too confusing to me. I was never satisfied with Catholicism. I stopped going to church at age seventeen, but I was still praying to God as I had from very early childhood.

♣I was a Baptist and I was attending Catholic school. I was very involved with the activities of the family church, but I can't say that I had any real commitment. As a teenager, I was constantly searching for what was correct.

♣For many years I "bounced around" from one Christian church to another. I was not happy at any of them. If something didn't work out with one church, I'd go to another. I thought that's all there was. Eventually, I became disenchanted with the whole idea. All I had seen were hypocrites, anyway, so I stopped attending church all together. I then entered the darkest phase of my life. I literally sank to the bottom of society.

These women were discontent with what they found at church and were questioning and searching for something to fill their spiritual void. There was a sense of readiness on their part for that which would meet the religious and spiritual needs they felt.

Women Who Came from a Mode of Commitment

For many of the women, religion was at the heart of their faith journey in their growing-up years. They were active participants in the church as teachers, pianists, soloists, and worshippers and felt deeply devoted to God and the religious aspect of their lives.

❖I was born and raised the daughter of a Nazarene minister and was very active in church musically. I was the church pianist for years and played and sang in many local contests.

❖I was raised a Baptist, but studied different religions after leaving home. I was raised in a Christian family that tried to live as Christians, not just pay lip service.

❖I grew up Catholic. For most of my youth I wanted to be a nun. I even spent time with the parish priest and even contacted a convent for information. I can say I was a devoted Catholic, attended daily mass—the whole works.

❖Prior to my conversion I was a Christian, going to Sunday school from two years of age and also attending church services with my family every Sunday from about six years of age. I was very devout and was baptized at age eight after being questioned by the minister of our church. At first he was skeptical to baptize someone so young, but after I answered all his questions, he decided that I was ready to become a formal member of the church. I was baptized and remained a faithful member until I met my husband. Then I began to study Islam.

✦Until eighteen years of age, I was a Methodist. At eighteen, I became a Catholic. Prior to that conversion I had read about all world "religions." I was very active in both denominations and other churches—to the point of receiving awards, medals, certificates, etc. I considered myself very active and religious. I wanted to become a nun. I knew several sisters in a local convent and inquired about nunnery life.

For many of these women, religion was a natural way of life. They were often dissatisfied with the answers they received to the questions they asked of church leaders. They were at "that phase" in life when they were trying to decide for themselves who they were and what they wanted their lives to be like; they were young adults making independent choices. It was at that point of searching that they made contact in some way with Islam.

3. CHANGING PATHS
American Women Choosing to Become Muslim

We were with Jodi for two days one summer attending a friend's wedding. She and Reza had been married for two years and were studying at the University of Arkansas, about an eight-hour drive from our home. She seemed so different, yet I liked her mature manner and her kindness. When making a hair appointment, she was careful to insist on a female rather than a male beautician. Even though it was in the middle of a hot summer, she wore long sleeves. Her conversation was serious as she spoke of what she was learning about Islam.

On the way to the wedding, we talked. Jodi sat with her dad in the front seat. She turned around to look at me sitting in the backseat and said, "Mom, who do you believe Jesus was?"

"Well, Jodi, you know. You've been going to church all your life," I replied.

"But, Mom, I want to hear you tell me now."

And so I told her what I thought was basic to the Christian belief of Jesus' birth, of his ministry, of his being the Son of God, of his death and resurrection for our salvation.

"Then Jesus is God?" Jodi asked.

"Yes, Jesus is part of the Trinity," I replied, "and throughout his teaching and ministry, he points us toward God."

I felt frustrated. Somehow her responses left me feeling inadequate. Why couldn't I do better? Even though she didn't say so, I could feel her moving toward an Islamic viewpoint. *Well, no chance of her going all the way,* I comforted myself.

All too soon Jodi was gone again, back into the world of university studies with her husband, Reza. We, too, returned to our home and jobs. We kept in touch with Jodi by phone. With each call, we felt the gap widening. She was a natural at imitating others and often sounded like an Iranian trying to learn English as she imitated her friends' accents. She talked of cooking—not American foods but Iranian cuisine. She spoke only of her Muslim friends—not Christian or even American friends. We couldn't quite define it, but there was a shift.

November came and Jodi and Reza came home for Thanksgiving. We had been apprehensive but looked forward to it. We really loved those two, and we missed them. Jodi came through the door. She was wearing a long dress over her jeans and sweater. She carried a scarf in her hand, and her hair was flat against her head. We embraced, then sat and talked in a rather stilted, surface manner. It was late and time to retire. Reza went out to carry in the suitcases. As I got up, Jodi came over by me.

"Mom, I need to talk to you."

I turned my back and headed for the kitchen. Tears were welling up in my eyes. No, I wouldn't talk with her. I couldn't stand what I thought she had to say. "Not now," I answered without looking at her.

The next day was Thanksgiving. We were all heading to Grandma's house, an hour's drive away. "Mom, we won't be eating the turkey or dressing. We're only eating approved meats."

Well, big deal! See if I care! I wouldn't look at or acknowledge her. She had the long dress on over her jeans again, and as we walked out the door, she put on the scarf so it covered all her hair. I sat in the front seat and sulked the entire trip. The rest of the family seemed to carry on as usual—Reza and Jodi, her two brothers, and her dad. I managed to avoid her the whole day until that night back at the house.

"Mom, we have to talk."

"I don't want to hear it."

"You've got to hear it, Mom, please." I finally gave in, and we sat down.

"Mom, I've converted to Islam. I was already Muslim this summer, but I wasn't ready to tell you then. I needed to grow stronger before I told you."

❖ ❖ ❖

The signs are often there that our young adults are changing from the path we want for them, yet we aren't sure just what to do about it. Consequently, we frequently ignore it, hoping the whole situation will go away, and we won't have to deal with it. As young adults, our children are beyond our control; they encounter many new ideas and new perspectives in the world, and they make their own decisions.

Daughters Learning of a New Path

Of the respondents to the questionnaire, 63 percent were married to Muslims before their conversions. Their attitudes toward Islam at the time of marriage ranged from fear of Islam to having already investigated Islam on their own. Twenty-three percent converted before marriage and later met and married a Muslim, while 6 percent who converted are still single. Only one woman responded as having become Muslim even though married to a white, American, non-Muslim male.

None of these women felt compelled by their husbands to study Islam and convert. In many instances it was the searching of the wife that drew the husband back into practice of his religion. These Muslim men (often not practicing) seemed, for the most part, to be well-versed in their religion. It wasn't a case of not knowing what Islam was and what it required; it was being away from family in a land where it was difficult to practice Islam that fostered less involvement. Family responsibilities and a searching, supportive wife naturally drew them again into the practice of their faith.

Although the stories of these women vary in the specifics, there are many commonalities in their introduction and conversion to Islam. The majority of women were introduced to Islam by the husband. Others were introduced by classes they took in college, and a few by acquaintance with Muslim neighbors or from having visited in an Islamic country. Islam touched in them a need they felt. Each in her own way chose to accept Islam and make shahada, declaring herself as Muslim by acknowledging "There is no God but Allah and Muhammad is a messenger of Allah." The following stories help us gain a sense of the variety of ways they learned about Islam and the conversion experiences that brought these women to the point of declaration.

The Witness of the Significant Other

The desire to further a relationship with a Muslim who had become a significant other was a motivator for some to investigate Islamic beliefs more seriously.

❖I met my husband in 1983. Prior to that I held all the common stereotypes of Islam, that it was medieval, subjugated women, and was violent. I never had any formal exposure to Islam despite a master's level education. Although not practicing the prayers or fasting regularly, my husband was very sure that Islam was the true religion of God. I was aware that although I was under no obligation to convert, he would not marry me without my committing to raise any children we would have as Muslims. I felt he had a sound value system and my initial exposure to the Qur'an did not convince me one way or the other, but I saw nothing I felt adverse about in raising our children Muslim.

In 1988, our first son was 18 months old. Our marriage was in deep trouble for a variety of reasons. I turned to the Qur'an to find ways I could use it to manipulate my husband into counseling. Our conflict reached a zenith in September, 1988, and I asked him for a separation. I felt I had no options, even though I still loved him. I was calm driving to work. Out of my soul came an intense pain, and I cried out loud for God to help me. At that moment I recognized my desire to be Muslim, and it did not matter if my marriage broke up or not. I wanted to be Muslim for me.

✣I met my husband at Louisiana Tech University. He didn't want to have an illegal relationship with me, so he immediately proposed marriage, asked me if I was interested in reading about Islam and becoming Muslim, and he actually asked me to put a cover on my hair.

I was insulted by the last two requests, and at eighteen, I wasn't sure I wanted to get married. I was attracted to him and wanted to be with him. He discontinued contact with me. I went home and read on my own about Islam. I changed and wanted to marry him.

✣[From one who was unchurched] My husband was supportive in helping me put my life together. I was recovering once again from emotional problems. He really had very little to do with my conversion. He introduced me to Islam but never asked me to convert. Islam does not require me to, but he returned fully to his religion. As I saw him gradually acquire an inner peace, I became envious. Inner peace was what I sought. So I asked for literature. The more I read, the more I wanted to learn. Islam means "submission to the will of God" or "inner peace." I felt God himself was leading me.

Learning About Islam in an Islamic Country

Some of the women actually visited Muslim countries and were profoundly affected by the people and their practice of Islam. They observed the lifestyles and the norms as lived out in an Islamic-based culture.

❖When I was eighteen I married my boyfriend because he was going to Vietnam. I decided to enlist in the Medical Corps. Around that time I was studying Judaism [although a Christian at the time], mainly because they did not believe in the Jesus as Savior thing. But I found out I did accept Jesus as a prophet and the Jews did not! I also accepted the virgin birth, which was another no-no, but everything else about their beliefs was okay with me—much different than the arguments I had with pastors and priests before, so I sort of considered myself a Jew-non-Jew type person.

I was a trained combat nurse and was present during the last days before Saigon fell in Vietnam. (Yes! A bona fide Vietnam veteran with a bronze star and 2 purple hearts!) In 1978 I was sent to Saudi Arabia because the United Nations needed trained personnel to conduct a relief campaign for immunization and care of the cholera epidemic sweeping through south Saudi Arabia, Oman, and Yemen regions. Many children were dying as well as old people. When I could, I watched the Bedouins pray several times a day and the only word I could make out was "Allah," but the devotion of those people impressed me.

I took a tour of the Middle East in early 1980 with my husband. In Cairo my "light bulb" went from dim to bright as I continued my study of Islam. My marriage was in the process of ending and when the divorce came, I had a nervous breakdown because my family and my husband's [family] were trying to "deprogram" me from this dangerous, religious "cult" I had become fascinated with. I buckled under and simply cracked from the confusion.

After intense therapy, I moved south to return to college and finish my half-completed bachelor's degree. There I met many Muslim students who wondered at my knowledge of their religion. Six months later I was reading the Qur'an full-time and took my shahada during Ramadan in 1989.

❖My conversion started when I took a religion class at Purdue University. This first introduction to Islam struck my mind and made more sense (and later, total sense) than other religions I studied. Then I decided to join a study summer tour to Egypt to visit a Muslim country firsthand, to see the mosques, to talk with the people. This opened my mind tremendously. From that point on, Islam was the only way for me to go. When I got back from Egypt, I went to the local mosque, and the sisters helped me begin my path of knowledge and life. In November 1993 I converted and have found peace in my life. Before converting I was not religious. I was drinking and being "wild." Islam taught me that this life is the judgment for the after-life and pleasing Allah (SWT) is most important.

❖I studied Islam as part of my college major in African and Middle Eastern Studies. . . . I did not believe anyone could truly practice Islam in the present age.

I traveled to West Africa as a volunteer and stayed 3 months. In that time, I met true Muslims. When they heard the call to prayer, they ran to the mosque. If someone had extra money beyond his basic needs, he gave it to someone less fortunate. The name of Allah was always on their tongues. The more I was with them, the more I wanted to embrace Islam.

I became very sick and had to be evacuated to a hospital in the capital. I had no one to comfort me—all my friends were far away. All I could do was pray. I prayed almost constantly for three days. I remembered the conversion story of Yusuf Islam (Cat Stevens); he was drowning and promised God he would devote his life to God if God spared his life. I did the same. Within two days, I was back in the village with my Muslim friends, but I still resisted converting.

I was miserable when I returned to the U.S. I could no longer function in a society so far removed from what I wanted. I met many American and Arab Muslims who encouraged me ever so gently to let go and submit to Allah. I became so exhausted from trying to resist the pull of Islam that finally on January 21, 1989, I converted.

These women seemed to have a fascination with what they observed in the Islamic countries. They were moved by what they saw and felt, and they responded by becoming part of that which was introduced to them.

The Witness of Muslim Neighbors and Acquaintances

Some of the young women met Muslims in this country who influenced them by their daily living and practice. They sensed in the Muslims personal strength that seemed to come from their beliefs. Sometimes the Muslims' witness was verbal as they responded to questions, but more often it was how they chose to live their lives.

❖I was fifteen years old when I first started to learn about Islam. A Saudi family moved in next door, and I was fascinated by their behavior, dress, language, and religion. The wife and I became very close, but it took four years for me to convert. They never pushed it on me; they simply answered my questions and showed me great kindness and hospitality. All throughout high school, though I was not a Muslim, I stayed away from negative elements. It came from my Saudi friends' influence. So when I converted, the only real things I changed were my clothing and leisure time activities such as concerts, movies, and sports.

❖Before becoming Muslim, I was an atheist and had withdrawn from the church; however, I wasn't closed toward long and in-depth discussions about God and this world. After several years of satisfying but "burn-out" type working, I started traveling through South Central America and ended up in Texas. A Muslim community welcomed me to stay and sort out my total and utterly miserable confusion. By the will of Allah, I was guided toward becoming Muslim, saying the shahada, and wanting to be married. This then settled me into a new identity and a different life orientation but without totally losing the old "me."

❖My husband wasn't practicing his religion at the time I met him so he had no objections when I decided to go back to church and take the kids. The only thing he requested was that we eat no pork. Visitors from Egypt to my father's business let me see for the first time Islam in full practice. It was then that my husband began to think about putting it in his life more seriously.

Then my aunt married a Muslim, and I spent much time there asking questions about Islam. In 1990 I gave birth to my fourth child, and I was caught unaware in my belief. What I mean is I really didn't know I believed in Islam. But one night Allah made the truth to hit me. It felt like a rock, and I cried like my three-week-old daughter that night as I sat staring at my plaque of the Lord's Prayer.

I kept my belief a secret even from my husband for another two weeks. I told him on the phone one day when he called me from work. He immediately started asking me why. He told me it was very serious, that I shouldn't "hop on to it." One must be convinced and not compelled. He cut me short saying "We'll talk about it when I get home." He later told me after he hung up the phone, he cried and thanked God. He promised to try to begin a new life and practice Islam to the full extent. He told me that night, he whispered the call to prayer in our newborn's right ear and the readiness call in her left—something he had not done with our other children.

✦In 1983, through friends I met an Arab woman, and we became best friends. One day she asked if I could babysit her daughters, and I did. One night before the kids went to bed they told me their prayers and also wanted to teach me. The next day, she asked me if I considered Jesus the Son of God. I replied, "Really, I have no religion but tell me more about your religion, Islam." It took me two more years from then to say shahada.

✦I volunteered to help tutor Saudi women who were studying English as a second language. I found it odd that these women refused to have a man tutor them, but after checking out and reading several books on Islam from the public and school libraries, I began to understand these "mysterious" ladies in black. The women began to open up more and more and invited me into their homes and my knowledge of Islam unfolded. I really respected the religion as I saw it practiced on a daily basis.

It was in the spring of 1988 that I really began to practice. I contacted the local Islamic Association and joined a sister's Qur'an study group. There I met sisters who were and still are great role models and guiding forces for me yet today.

The impact of devout and dedicated Muslims on the lives of these women supports the church growth principle that in Christianity most are converted to a church because of someone they know who influences their lives toward accepting Christ and the church. These women sensed that living as a Muslim fulfilled these people spiritually and they, too, wanted to feel very close to God by being a true Muslim.

Learning About Islam in the College Setting

Many of the women made contact with Islam for the first time in the college setting. It may have been through specific religion courses, books they read for general college classes, or Muslim students or friends they associated with on campus. Hearing about Islam greatly interested them.

❖I was meeting with a group of international students as part of a conversation group program to practice English. As I listened to a Palestinian man talk about his life, his family, his faith, it struck a nerve in me. The more I learned about Islam the more I became interested in it as a possibility for my own life.

The following term the group disbanded, but I registered for a class "Introduction to Islam." This class brought back all the concerns I had about Christianity. As I learned about Islam, all of my questions were answered. All of us are not punished for Adam's original sin. Adam asked God for forgiveness and our merciful and loving God forgave him. God doesn't require a blood sacrifice in payment for sin. We must sincerely ask for forgiveness and amend our ways. Jesus wasn't God; he was a prophet like all the other prophets. They all taught the same message: believe in the One true God, worship and submit to God alone, and live a righteous life according to the guidance he has sent.

This answered all my questions about the Trinity and the nature of Jesus (all God, all human, or a combination?). God is a perfect and fair judge, who will reward or punish us based on our faith and righteousness. I found a teaching that put everything in its proper perspective, and appealed to my heart and intellect. It seemed natural. It wasn't confusing. I had been searching. I found a place to rest my faith.

❖I was in college taking psychology and sociology but felt a need to turn back to religion even though I didn't agree with Christianity a whole lot, especially the way it had been presented to me before in life. After shopping around at all the different religions like Hinduism, Buddhism, I enrolled in the religious studies class in college and took literature of the Old Testament. One of the things that came up was going back to look at the roots of Christianity. It seemed that Christianity was okay then, but it got changed to the point to where women were not really accepted, as well as other changes. Reading through the texts, I came across things that the pastors in our church had never talked about. It really shook me, and it made me begin to question the Bible.

My husband gave me a Qur'an as a wedding gift, and it just sat on the shelf during the time I was taking the religion classes. After that we went to Syria to visit the family. I couldn't speak the language so I had a lot of time on my hands. So I read the whole thing, and while reading it I was looking for things that seemed incorrect or were problems to me. I came across things in the English translation that bothered me, like "Lightly beat your wife." So I would say to my husband, "How can you believe this stuff?" Then he would say, "No, in Arabic that's not the way it really is," and would explain from the original. I went through the whole thing and couldn't find anything inaccurate. And I thought, "Well, this is better than anything else I've seen." I converted in 1988.

❖I was Roman Catholic. I studied African-American studies as part of my work toward a degree in social sciences. After reading *The Autobiography of Malcolm X*, I felt compelled to understand the power behind Brother Malcolm's transformation after making hajj, when he returned to the U.S. and said that racism is not a part of Islam. As I began to study, I felt certain that lightning would strike me down for studying another religion. I studied casually for three months, intensely for the next three months, then made shahada to Allah before I first stepped into a masjid for the first time on May 29, 1993. On May 30, 1993, I made shahada in front of witnesses in the masjid.

The change was not a choice for me; it was going home. It gave me answers to questions I'd had and questions I didn't have. I love Islam. I love the concept of ummah. Alhamdulillah, that Allah has seen me fit to test.

Searching to Fill the Spiritual Void

Many of the respondents were searching for something in the spiritual area to fill the void in their lives. It was through this openness that many began to receive the pull toward Islam. This need is reflected in most of the descriptions the women give of their conversion experience. They may have come to the conversion point from a variety of situations, but most were receptive because of the need within themselves and the gentle persuasion of the Muslim person or resource which touched their hearts and souls.

❖I married someone who was not a Christian and we both were non-practicing in anything religious. I still thought of myself as a Christian. "What else is there," I thought. I still held my belief of God and his creation of the earth, but wasn't sure of the other beliefs I was taught growing up.

The year after my divorce in 1990 I started thinking about what I needed, about what I believed. Early in 1991 I started checking books out of the library and reading about Islam, more because I was curious about it than anything. I slowly read books on it, but also lived my life as I had been living it. It wasn't until the fall of 1992 that I decided I had to do something about it—either get serious about studying it or forget about it. I found several American Muslim sisters in Manhattan, twenty miles from where I lived in a very small town. I studied with them and learned the practical aspects of what I had read for the past year and a half. I took my shahada in December 1992.

❖My struggle began many years ago with my search for self-identity. Growing up in America as a black presented meaningful challenges to me during the 1960s and 1970s. After rallying around certain racial issues and feeling the pressures of early integration in Mississippi and Texas, I began to question my "role" in life as a black woman.

I was a successful professional, but my personal life was a mess. Bad marriage, poor relationship with parents and siblings, discontented with church and God—these all led me to question who I was and why and what I could do to improve relationships with these people and the world in general.

I began to seek out answers by researching black history. I was amazed to find out that most African people came from Islamic states. I later met some Sunni Muslims who shared very impressive information about heaven and hell that touched my Sufi heart. I was teaching speech and drama at a Catholic high school in Washington, D.C. at the time.

I became Muslim in 1974. I was asked to resign at the end of the year because several students also converted to Islam.

Islam cooled me out. It helped me to find God without all of the hangups and guilt I felt as a Christian. I've always loved God, and knowing that I could talk directly to Allah was a welcoming treat.

❖I was first introduced to Islam at the age of fourteen, but because of family conflicts I was not able to learn or practice. After leaving home to go to college, I had the freedom to pursue the religion. The biggest change I had to make (besides the obvious ones of dress, diet, etc.) was to put some distance between myself and my family and former friends. I did this as a protection for myself that would allow me to grow stronger in my religion without distractions. I had little sense of loss because I filled the void with newfound Muslim friends, and later, my husband.

Sensing the Authority of the Qur'an

Many of the women have expressed their growing respect and love for the Qur'an, which is considered the final and literal word of God. For some women the Qur'an was an important part of their conversion experience.

❖My conversion began as the result of a challenge by a Muslim to read the Qur'an in order for us to have a debate on the position of women in Islam. I held the stereotypical view of Muslim women as being oppressed and in a bad position relative to their Christian counterparts. I was nominally Christian, raised in a Catholic environment, but was not practicing the religion and really only bothered to label myself a Christian in order not to appear too rebellious in front of my extended family (my family was also really only Christian in name, not "reality").

The reading of the Qur'an and of hadith of the Prophet is what captured me. I went through a very odd experience whereby for the whole week it took me to read the Qur'an I couldn't sleep and seemed to toss and turn all night in a feverish sweat. I had strange and vivid dreams about religious topics, and when I would get up all I wanted to do was continue reading the Qur'an. I didn't even study for my final exams which were happening at the same time!

❖I began a course in Middle Eastern History, which immersed me further into the study of Islam. When the professor read passages from the Qur'an to illustrate how powerful a "tool" it was in spreading Islam throughout the world, my heart sang. I knew I had found the TRUTH! I had been searching for God since the early '80s. At this point I knew I would someday be a Muslim. After the class was over I continued my investigation into Islam. I bought an English translation of the Qur'an and read it daily. I was living at home at the time so hid most of this from my family. I got together often with my new friends and my total lifestyle began to change.

❖My conversion was a long process. I left Christianity while in junior high school. I was raised Methodist. My father had been a minister one time and was rather strict when I was a child. My parents left the church—mother went the American Indian Lakota way and father just left. I looked into a number of faiths but nothing attracted me. I was raised to look at other cultures from a point of understanding to try to step out of my own culture to view others. The Iranian revolution sparked many questions for me. I decided to learn more about the people and culture and began reading the history of Iran which led to history of Islam—an area not even touched in school. This led to reading Qur'an. I hit an emotional crisis when a relationship (with an Arab) fell apart, and I found myself turning to the Qur'an. I realized a need to rely on something other than people. My mother was dead, my family far away. I didn't know who I could turn to or trust. The Qur'an touched a chord. I got in touch with a [Muslim] women's study group and they were very supportive and informative. I especially liked Islam's base of logic. It took me a year to finally take shahada.

This holy book, the Qur'an, so revered by Muslims as the final word of God and *the* direction for humankind, touched these women as if it were a call to the faithful to come and submit themselves to that which is holy and divine. They responded with zeal and passion to Islamic scripture.

Finding Answers in Islam

Some of the women tried to prove Christianity to their Muslim husbands. They sought help from Christian leaders but were frustrated in their attempts. Some of the women struggled with letting go of Christianity even though they felt "Muslim." Several religious questions seemed unsettling to them. Whereas Islam tends to "have the answers," there is often confusion in Christian theology. In Islam there is only one God so how can Jesus also be God, the Muslims ask.

The Bible, viewed by many Christians as being the literal word of God, is also questioned. Muslims emphasize the many changes made over the centuries in the numerous manuscripts that make up the Bible and that it was written by those who only "felt inspired," often many years after the events occurred. They point out what they feel are contradictions in the Bible.

Muslims are well-versed in their beliefs and are often able to fill in the gaps for the confused person longing for God, for answers, for what to do to be at peace. Varying degrees of dissatisfaction with Christian theology as they perceive it is apparent in many of these women's stories. Some of the problems center in the concepts of Trinity, original sin, or Jesus as the Son of God or Jesus as God. Their frustration with some of these ideas helped to open the door for a "new" religious expression.

❖After the birth of our second child, I decided to go back to church. I was so enthusiastic and went around singing, reading the Bible, and telling my husband how much he should get back to God. With some reluctance he went to church with me and my daughter several times.

One day he said, "I can't go anymore and I don't want you to take our daughter either." We had a big fight and were going to split up until we decided that we would take a look at both religions. If I could explain Christianity satisfactorily, he would become a Christian. At the same time, I would take another look at Islam. (I had claimed Islam two years after we were married, but he wasn't active and I lost interest quickly.)

I started asking a lot of questions from ministers, theologians, and seniors in the field to help me prove Christianity to my husband. I wanted it so badly, I cried to several of them to help me and most of them said, "I'm sorry—I don't know" or "I'll write you," but I never heard from them. The harder I tried to prove Christianity to convert him, the more I moved toward Islam because of its logic, until I finally yielded to the belief and oneness of Allah.

One thing led to another until my husband and I became practicing Muslims. Islam for me gives me peace of mind because I don't have to understand the Trinity and how God is "three in one" or that God died on the cross. For me Islam supplies the answers.

❖I called myself agnostic when I went to college. I thought I believed in God and didn't want to do anything about it. After a few years, I was ready to go back to being "religious" again. In the meantime, I met a man from Lebanon who would later become my husband. He and I both started learning more about Islam and about six months later I converted. We were married six months after that. The hardest part was changing my ideas about Jesus. It took a long time to be able to say that Jesus isn't the Son of God without it feeling like blasphemy. But I realized that the beliefs are really close in some ways. Mary was a virgin and Jesus is a great prophet. The difference is in the divinity of Jesus.

✤I never knew anything about Islam except that "Muhammad was a killer and Islam was spread by the sword." I was going out with my husband prior to marriage (he was not a practicing Muslim at that time), but when we got married and he finally told his family, his father's stipulation was that I was to be Muslim. I told him I could not change my religion for a man because I have always been close with God but never had a direct path to walk. Then I started talking about what I really believed. I promised God that I would look into Islam, and I asked God to guide me.

Over the course of several months I started talking to my husband's friend who had embraced Islam and was a humble practicing Muslim. I asked him many questions. I kept away from my husband about this topic because I wanted to be as objective as possible. My hardest hurdle was getting over the fiery images of what we would look like burning up in hell from my Sunday school books and training. I had been told so many times that if I did not believe Jesus had died for my sins and was my personal savior I would go to hell forever. But Allah showed me the way. I was reading many books about Islam, and everything I read was exactly how I felt inside me. All the answers were there. I may not have understood everything but what I did made sense. I embraced Islam and shared my first Ramadan with my husband of six months who was now practicing his beliefs.

The idea that Jesus is considered God by Christians was something that hadn't become a reality to some of the women. Muslims were, therefore, able to refute this belief by affirming that putting anything or anyone on the same level as God is a great sin. This point is probably the most dividing belief between Christians and Muslims. For Christians it would be a great sin to deny Jesus as part of the Trinity; for Muslims the greatest sin would be to place Jesus (whom they consider as a revered and great prophet) on the level of God.

❖I asked my friend to attend Mass with me. He said he didn't attend church, that he was a Muslim. "What's a Muslim?" I asked, totally unaware that my life was going to change forever as soon as he began his answer. At first, I listened intently but after he got to the part which denied Jesus being the Son of God, even denied his sacrifice for us on the cross, I excused myself from this friend and kicked myself for wasting so much time that now I had missed Mass and would have to go to confession.

We talked again later about his beliefs. We seemed more and more alike in our belief: heaven and hell, angels, our duty to our fellow man, holy scriptures. It was just the "Jesus thing" that kept us on opposite ends of the spectrum. I also noticed another complication; despite everything, I was falling in love with him.

It wasn't Islam that was the issue. It was Christianity. I was a "doubting Thomas" in every way and the guilt was overwhelming. I began to seek all kinds of advice to rid me of this demon of doubt. Then, three events took place in the space of a week that caused me to decide to leave Christianity altogether.

First, I went to a nun that I trusted deeply and poured my heart out. She responded with compassion, but she handed me a Qur'an as I left. I was very confused. Then, I went to my religion teacher, who was a lay person. As we talked, I grew more confused and finally said, "Look, I just want you to tell me that, undoubtedly and with full conviction, Jesus Christ is the Son of God." He didn't look at me when he said, "I can't tell you that." Now I was angry too. What was wrong with these people that they refused to give me the answers I was looking for?

Finally, I turned to God. At least I was sure that he was still there for me. And he would help me. I prayed that he would open my mind and my heart and show me the answer I was looking for. I used a method I had used many times before. I would pray everything in my heart, then open the Bible to a random page and find my answer. I opened my Bible to the trial of Jesus in front of Pontius Pilate. Pilate was trying to get Jesus to say something by which he could be convicted, in order to relieve his own guilt for having him sentenced to death to fulfill the wishes of the people. Pilate asked him, "Are you the Son of God?" and Jesus answered, in Matthew, Mark, Luke and John, "It is you who have said it." Suddenly, I felt at peace.

❖When I was eighteen I went to a local two-year Christian college. It was there that I first came in contact with Muslims. There were a lot of them there, and I was fascinated with the idea of another group of people I knew nothing about—some people from the "Holy Land." I took a course called "The World's Living Religions" and learned a little about Islam. I met my husband-to-be there when I was nineteen years old. I married him after four months.

We moved far away to go to a university. There I met an American-Muslim woman who wore hijab. She gave me books and pamphlets about Islam. I read some of them and watched some debates between Muslims and Christians about the divinity of Jesus and the authenticity of the Bible.

It was then that I heard clearly for the first time that the Christians (including the Catholics) thought that Jesus was God and that the Bible had been changed by men and mostly made by men's words, not God's. I was shocked. I knew then that I was not one of "them" anymore.

Finding Something Familiar in Islam

The close identity of Islam with the prophets, with the emphasis on Allah as the same God the Christians and Jews worship, with the acceptance of Jesus as a great prophet and teacher, with the tracing of their roots to Abraham—all these make a familiar setting into which Prophet Muhammad came to bring the final word, to set right with direct revelation God's word of "the way" to the people.

This familiarity may have been part of the easy transition for some of the American-born women when Muslim beliefs were explained.

❖After meeting my husband we shared our religious beliefs, which were similar. I began exploring my religious feeling after he asked me about my beliefs of Jesus being God, and he explained about prophethood and Muhammad. I agreed with these Islamic interpretations. I began studying from interest about Islam. Six months after we had married I began doing the prayers. After another six months, I participated in the fast during Ramadan. I found at this point that Islam defined my belief. I could no longer deny my belief in Islam just to prevent hurting people's feelings.

❖When I met the man who would become my husband and learned that he was Muslim, I was scared and asked all the questions that caused my fear. I also took a course in college called "Islam and Social Change" and learned even more about Islam. As I learned more and more in the course, the more questions I had and the more afraid I became. This fear, however, was different than the fear of the unknown; this fear was a fear of self-discovery. I found that all along I shared the beliefs taught through Islam but never had a name for it. This course, the *Qur'an,* and my husband helped me realize that for a number of years I had been living a Muslim life without knowing it. (It wasn't until I learned the Five Pillars of Islam that I began completely practicing as a Muslim.) So when people ask how long I have been a Muslim I can't tell them, but I can think that it has been eleven years. If they ask me when I converted, I can tell them in 1992. As a matter of fact, my husband knew before I did that I was Muslim but let me come to that realization on my own.

And so began the faith journey for these women that would affect those around them—the families in which they were raised, their friends, their colleagues at work or school. Most of all, it would change the direction and flow of their own lives, not just in a religious sense but in every facet of their existence.

4. FORSAKING
THE PREVIOUS PATH
Reactions of Relatives

odi and I sat in the family room that evening on Thanksgiving Day, just the two of us. At last I knew I *had* to listen. I wanted to be sure I could go over at a later time what she would say to me—this was important! I knew I was too emotionally distraught to be logical, so I set up the tape recorder to record our conversation. The following excerpts are taken from that recorded conversation between Jodi and me.

She began. "Last July I decided to change to Islam, not drastic at first but this last month I decided to wear the cover. So I wear it every day, and it is my own choice. This was all on my own. Reza is happy about it, but he didn't ask me to do it. I wanted to tell you and let you ask any questions you have. I have chosen this for me. I will help you work it through, if you want to work it through. That is all I can offer. I'm willing to take all the nasty comments or whatever you want to dish out. It's not going to be easy for me to be on the 'wrong' side . . . although I don't feel like either of us is on the wrong side; we just have made different choices. I have other things I want to say, but I'd like to hear your expression."

I responded. "I'm very hurt because of this. There were several things I asked you to do and wanted you to do—to hear about Christianity from an adult point of view, from someone who really knows. I feel that you made no effort to do that. I'm very disappointed you didn't follow through on that. I am very angry and have been for a long time. For the last few months it has been like you are dying and slipping away from us. It's like we are in constant grieving."

"Mom, this is my own decision. It is not a rejection of you. I don't want to hurt you; I feel like I can express myself through this. I've come a long way from what I was."

"What do you expect from us as parents?"

"I don't know that I expect anything. Maybe it's the fact that I'm not going to be around. I don't even know how long my life is going to be. Maybe it's just a dream, but I have been feeling like there are certain things I have to do in Islam. I have asked other people if they have these feelings and they say no. They have hopes and dreams, but mine is more a feeling that I have a certain way to go. My life may be hard and I will have to be a strong person, but if I am strong enough I can make it."

"So how do we fit into your life, Jodi?" I asked.

"I see you as being very far away, and I see you as being the building blocks for what I am."

"I feel like you are saying what you have had—what we have given you—is not good enough, and you are going to junk all that and reject everything about us. You're breaking all your ties like you don't care about anything in the past."

"Mom, I first felt that when I was at our church youth camp as a teenager. They were talking about how the disciples laid down everything and followed Jesus, and the material things were not that important; they even left their families. I started to think there were so many things I couldn't give up. I couldn't give up my records—I loved to play them. I was soul-searching at that point. No, I couldn't give up several things. It would surely take a strong person to give things up and go follow Jesus in that way. No, I could never do that, and I was sad about it. But then there came a time when I realized that for once in my life I didn't care about the material things, that other things were more impor-tant—the spiritual life and relationships."

We continued to talk. I harangued her about the drastic change of wearing hijab. I made insulting remarks about her sloppy clothes and scarf. Over and over I accused her of rejecting us.

She tried to affirm to me over and over, "I am not rejecting you. I'm only doing things in a different way. . . . You and Dad are my models. I love the way you help people and counsel with those in need. . . . I've chosen a different way. All I can do is help you deal with it."

Finally I lost control and broke down crying. "I'm just crushed. I never would have thought I'd react this way. I have worked so hard on how to accept all this, and I'm just not making it. I've suffered so much these past days. I just don't know what to do. I keep wondering where we went wrong, yet some of the things you're doing are fantastic. I don't want to lose you, yet I want to push you as far away from me as I can. If I didn't care so much, I'd want to never see you again. I hate it. But I'm going to keep working at it."

We clung to each other and cried for a long time. Then Jodi added, "Reza really loves and respects you and Dad. We have chosen a little different way, what we think is right, but we see you as good, strong people too. We hope our marriage can be as good as yours and that we will help people like you do. We are just very simple and have a lot of struggle as far as health and study and work—making everything hang together. But we want to keep working at it."

Finally, we had no more to say to each other. I went to my room, and I sobbed most of the night. Never have I experienced grief like that period of time. I hurt so much that it felt as if something was physically being pulled out of me. About noon the next day, I knelt at my bedroom window and prayed: "God of the Christians, the Muslims, the universe, what am I going to do? How can I stand this?" Then, as I sat back waiting for help, I heard the music my sons were playing in the next room—the Beatles singing "Yesterday, all my troubles seemed so far away./

Love was such an easy game to play./ Oh, how I long for yester-day!" I prayed, "God, that is just how I feel. I long for yesterday when it was so much easier with Jodi."

Then the Beatles sang another song: "Hey Jude, don't be sad; Take a sad song and make it better." That hit me because I wanted to take this sad song and make it a glad song. A positive feeling came over me. The healing process was beginning. When Jodi and Reza left to go back to Arkansas, I was able to put my arms around them and say: "I want to work it through. Please help me. I love you so much. I want my daughter back, and I'll learn to accept what you have chosen." I could not risk losing my daughter and son-in-law. I would do whatever it took to heal the relationship.

❖ ❖ ❖

Religious decisions are often among the most intense types of trauma in family life. Emotions run high, and reactions to such decisions lead to changes that may cause separation in families. The journey toward acceptance, if it occurs at all, may be long and arduous.

The respondents, sharing their personal stories about initial parental responses, reflect everything from acceptance to com-plete cutoff and rejection. Forty-six percent ranked their parents' responses at first as negative and stressful, while 23 percent indicated they were accepted in an "okay manner" without much stress and anger. Fourteen percent said their parents were very accepting and supportive. Some indicated it was not a choice for the parents to accept or reject; it was none of their business what their children chose to do as adults.

Over time, healing, where needed, has begun to take place in a majority of the families. Most of the women have seen great improvement in their relationships with and acceptance by family members although a few have been cut off with no relationship worked out. Sometimes physical distance works for them as a positive contribution to the relationship because they are not close enough to need to work through day-to-day contact. In other situations, however, the distance keeps the relationship frozen at the status quo with no movement toward resolution.

The women wrote of various reactions and stages that families may go through when faced with their daughter's choice to become Muslim.

Accepting the Choice

There are those families who were open and accepting to their daughter's choice to convert, especially after initial concerns were dealt with and the parents felt assurance that their daughters would be okay.

❖After my conversion, I presented myself wearing hijab. I explained myself to them. I never worried much about my family. I knew they would accept what I was happy with. I had one brother who would tease me and tell me to take off my scarf. I think it was easy for me to become Muslim because I knew I could depend on my family not to turn their back. I explained and answered questions freely. I gave my dad the Qur'an to read.

❖My choice to be Muslim has not affected my relationship with my family of origin. My mother is glad that I am a more religious person. She is happy for me. She doesn't know much about the Islamic religion, but she knows that I believe in the one and only God so she has been accepting of my conversion. We don't live close to my family of origin.

❖When I came to Islam and told my parents, my father was understanding and supportive. My mother was apprehensive. I feel she was apprehensive because of several factors: (1) her love for me and wanting the best for me; (2) the stereotypes associated with women's role in Islam; (3) a journey to Beirut [she made] when she was younger; and (4) a serious relationship she had with a Muslim man. I think my mom wanted me to be certain of all aspects of the religion before I made a decision. Most mothers want the best for their children and want to protect them, and we all are aware of the attitude toward Islam in today's society. I would like to stress that not once did my mom not support me in my decision; she only voiced her concerns, which is just what I was looking for when I told my parents—questions, concerns, and comments.

❖Unfortunately we haven't yet been able to visit my family in Switzerland (however, it is in our plans). They had to come to the United States when I converted and married. Once they had reassured themselves that I was okay, that my husband was lovable, they accepted my decision. Questions abound however. We probably will be talking a great deal. My prayer is to have my father become Muslim, since in his heart he already is.

❖I have no family of origin except a brother whom I haven't seen since long before my conversion. I think he is fairly pleased with my conversion because he can see that I am setting more realistic goals.

❖I have had no major problems with my family. They have accepted me as Muslim as long as it is what I want. Some of them think I'm crazy because I'm wearing the hijab and my husband acts more like an American. We have never gotten into any fights though. We spend as much time as we can with each other in person or by phone.

✤My family is okay with me. There was never any problem because I was quiet about my reasons for changing my lifestyle. My parents watched my attitude change in college. I came home with an Afro hairstyle, and they nearly died. I had the first divorce in the family. That was high on their no-no list. By the time they realized I had a life of my own, they just wished me the best and never have criticized me or Islam. They are just happy I believe in God and have kept good morals and values and passed them on to my sons.

These families were able to make the adjustment to accept their daughter's decision once they felt confident that she would be safe and understood to some extent the intentions and commitment. Perhaps these families were also the kind to let go and let their daughter be an individual with boundaries of her own whether or not she became Muslim. This does not mean there will not be future relationships to work out; family relationships are always in flux, shifting and repositioning as time and life go on.

Acceptance with Reservations

Seeing daughters embrace another religious tradition may leave family members feeling as if an unseen but deeply felt chasm separates them. This sense of separation is felt by brothers, sisters, grandparents, aunts, uncles, and friends although the level of acceptance varies among family members. Some may accept readily; others may not be able to be open at all. Brothers or sisters may be embarrassed to be seen in public with their sister's new mode of dress and cover. Grandparents may not understand how this beloved grandchild could make such a choice, but they may be the ones who maintain contact as may other extended family members.

Some families fear their daughter is going to hell for her denial of Christ. They are pushed theologically to work through the

Christian concept of salvation in regard to their daughter, and they struggle to find a satisfying level of comfort concerning this issue.

❖With the exception of my mother, my family took my conversion in stride. To this day I still feel as if she begrudges me for my decision to convert. I hope, insha'Allah, she can fully accept my lifestyle someday. Last fourth of July we had a picnic that turned ugly because we got on the subject of politics and the World Trade Center, which in turn came down to Christianity verses Islam. I resolved the situation by making it clear that if she was telling me to turn away from Islam, I would never see her again. She relented, but I feel she wasn't quite sincere.

❖I have a very small family, one sister. I don't have contact with my mother—my father raised both my sister and me. My sister is university-educated and has studied religions, so she totally accepted my decision to convert and accepted my marrying an Arab Muslim.

My father has had a harder time accepting it. He hasn't gone to church since before I stopped going, but he thinks that I should act "American," dress like everyone else, celebrate Christmas like everybody else—basically, not be different than others. But he is beginning to accept my life as a Muslim and that my daughter will be raised a Muslim.

❖My family always saw me as the "weird" one, so when I called and told them of my "new" religion, they just waited to see when I'd lose interest. Years later, my mother made comments about how I [had] changed and why I didn't stay in the religion I was raised in (we only went to church on Easter). She and my dad accept it, but I think my mom wishes I'd "go back." They especially dislike me staying home versus working, although they support my home school efforts. My parents are very hands-off. They accepted my first name [Muslim name] change easily.

My father seems more accepting, maybe even approving. He likes my dress (my mom is embarrassed) and has even read some of my books.

❖My parents were very upset when they first learned of my conversion. I think they hoped it was a "phase" I'd go through and grow out of. My dad read the whole Qur'an, my mom took a course in her church about Islam and so they both learned more about it and now feel more comfortable with it. I don't think they will ever become Muslim, but I hope they do. My sister is a fundamentalist Christian and refuses to talk about it. She is upset that I will be going to hell when I die and prays for me all the time. We have a good relationship otherwise, and it is understood that neither one of us should bring up religion unless we want to argue.

❖My relationship with my parents is fine. They are quite understanding about my conversion and are very open-minded. My grandmother is not very happy about me being a Muslim. She denied the fact that the local paper reported that I was a Muslim. She said it was a mistake and I told her it was not. I hope that someday my grand-mother will understand my desire to be a Muslim. The only stress is with my grandmother. I wish I could be open with her regarding my faith. I have no difficulties with my parents. In fact I love to visit them and even my grand-mother is fun to talk to if we leave religion out of the discussion.

❖They were very upset at first but now they reluctantly accept it. My father got very angry and twisted my arm and told me about my hijab, to "take that thing off because

I don't want to be seen with you in public." This happened in 1983.

I hope to remain close to them. But I also plan to live where the Muslims are, which will separate us by miles. I know Islam is against severing blood ties (a major sin mentioned in the Qur'an). I really love my mom, brothers, and sisters.

There is a tremendous struggle in adjusting relationships to find acceptable ways of relating with this daughter who has forsaken the parents' path and is so different now. The chasm is so wide and affects the relationship physically, emotionally, and spiritually. Despite the resistance at first to the daughter's changing path, there is a gradual acceptance and bridging of the separation. This bridging no doubt comes out of the intense need for love by the daughter for her family and the family's need to have their daughter close in relationship.

Working Toward Acceptance

Although families may have reacted with shock and grief at first, they were willing to work through their relationship with their daughter. Their willingness to work on the relationship was often motivated by other circumstances such as the birth of a baby to the Muslim couple. The movement toward acceptance may come with the passage of time, perhaps after the family of origin recognizes that what the daughter had chosen was not just a phase in her life. At times the commitment to work it out seems to come more from the daughter than from the family. Such drastic changes in lifestyles, religion, dress, and tradition made the husband an easy mark for some families to shift the blame from their daughter to her husband. Some of the women made the change to Islam while still living in their parents' home. All of these situations required time, effort, and work on the part of both the family and the daughter to come to some level of acceptance. These families are still working on that process of acceptance.

❖When I embraced Islam, I told my family. They were not surprised. They saw it coming from my actions and what I said when I was home that summer. They accepted my decision and knew that I was sincere. Even before, my family always accepted my activities and my deep faith, even if they didn't share it.

They were not as open-minded, however, when I started to wear the hijab. They worried that I was cutting myself off from society, that I would be discriminated against, that it would discourage me from reaching my goals, and they were embarrassed to be seen with me. They thought it was too radical. They didn't mind if I had a different faith, but they didn't like it to affect my life in an outward way.

It has been three years and a lot has changed. My family recognizes that I didn't destroy my life. They see that Islam has brought me happiness, not pain and sorrow. They are proud of my accomplishments and can see that I am truly happy and at peace. Our relationship is back to normal and they are looking forward to our visit next month, insha'Allah.

❖Upon becoming a Muslim, I felt that my parents were disappointed in me. Telling them that I was a Muslim was like a slap in the face to them. It was as if I had rejected everything they had taught me as a child—everything that they had learned from their parents. It was good enough for them, so why was it not good enough for me? My brothers were sixteen, fourteen, and eleven years old when I converted, and they were not really concerned about me. It was my choice and I had the right to do what I wanted. My other relatives are still friendly with me by telephone, but when my husband and I visit them in person, they seem tense and aloof, even ignoring us at times and talking to each other as if we were not even there. No one in my family has been interested in Islam and none of them want to become a Muslim.

My mother used to wish that my husband would go back to Iran and leave me behind. She imagined that I would then leave Islam and be the daughter she had before. After four years of marriage, my husband went overseas and returned about six weeks later. My mother realized he was not going to leave me and slowly began to accept my conversion to Islam.

Then I discussed my beliefs and practices with her, and she accepted me unconditionally. She realized I had chosen to believe as I do. She said she and my dad were too old to change their ways. After my thirteen years of marriage, she told me that I looked beautiful in my head scarf, just like the statues of the Virgin Mary.

When my brother, who is a minister, wrote me a letter and said that my husband, our little children, and I would be going to hell for our beliefs, my mother disagreed with him. She said that she believed there were several ways to get close to God and that she did not think we would go to hell. Five years later she passed away, may God grant her peace, and the last time I spoke to her she talked about not being afraid to die. She said she was not worried about me, but she did worry about my three brothers, including the Christian minister. She may have finally come to accept Islam as truthful even though she could not practice it herself.

❖My husband and I are in a unique situation because we both still live in my parents' house. They are very understanding and have not openly expressed any feelings against our beliefs, and my mother always takes care to only make pork for my father when we are eating out. We usually get together with my grandparents around holidays and they usually give us gifts. I learned from when I was a Jehovah's Witness not to try to "spoil their fun" by refusing gifts.

There have been small matters of difficulty such as fighting with my mother over the length of the clothes she makes for me. "Why do you want them so ridiculously long?!" and her frustration when I told her I could not eat food made with gelatin either (since it is usually made from pork). All in all, she has become more understanding over time, even realizing by herself that the American media purposely portrays Muslims in a bad light, now that she knows what we are really like.

I hope in the future we will be able to discuss more about our specific beliefs, which we haven't done much, and also discuss more with my father, who has basically no interest in religion of any kind.

❖Initially my conversion to Islam caused major conflicts with my family. They were not supportive and felt that I was being misguided and brainwashed by my husband. This later changed for two reasons: (1) they realized this wasn't a fad or change I was going through, and if they wanted to have any contact with me they would have to accept me as Muslim, and (2) once my children were born and being raised Muslim, it was hard for them to deal with the children in the same negative manner.

I've tried to speak to my family about Islam in hopes that I can help them to live and die as Muslims.

❖At first my mother and father were shocked. My father blamed my husband. Although the two had been the best of friends, after my conversion my father rarely spoke to my husband for an entire year. Many family squabbles have come out of my conversion. Most of the intolerance was on my mom's side of the family. To them I had become a devil worshipper who had denounced Christ. However, at a recent family reunion, I had been upgraded to a Christian who just didn't know [how] to accept and claim the healing of Christ. I've learned not to discuss religion with them.

Now my mom tells me what color of scarves look best on me and compliments me often. She has grown to accept it. I just wish my parents would ask me what I believe and read some of the Qur'an.

❖My choice to become a Muslim has made a difference in my relationship with my family—it is very stressful. I feel as though they think it's a stage of life I'm going through. It has been four years now and things are still a bit weird. I feel a little rejection. I would like for my family to be open with me and ask questions, instead of taking the facts of Islam from the media or other wrong sources. The most stressful thing I feel is that my family blames my husband for my conversion to Islam.

I like to be the best example of a Muslim when I visit my family, but I get very sad knowing they are not Muslims. My mom always tells me she wished my other two sisters were as good a mother as me. Being a good mom is part of being a good Muslim.

How fortunate were these women whose families made some effort at reconciliation and understanding. Often parents feel that decisions made by children in the young adult years are impulsive and frivolous. Although that is a possibility, time has demonstrated that the daughter's commitment is lasting and the change in her lifestyle is permanent.

Turning Their Backs on Acceptance

Some families seemed to be unable to tolerate the change. They felt safer by breaking off relationships completely or having very little to do with their daughter. For some of the converts, the lifestyle of the family of origin is so different from what their life as a Muslim requires that they have chosen to stay removed from the family. The family's lack of acceptance seems to stem from two basic problems: (1) a lack of understanding about the choice or (2) a refusal to understand the choice. Families may learn to get along on a surface basis but feel uncomfortable if it goes beyond that. Serious discussion may be difficult in these families, and an undercurrent of blame and hostility may be present.

❖Since I took my shahada, my family has grown farther apart from me in our relationship. I ask Allah (SWT) to give them guidance and the blessing that Allah (SWT) gave me—a future to work for in the hereafter. I hope for them to respect me and my religion. They thought the religious part was a cult and I would outgrow it, until they saw how serious I was and then had an arranged marriage. The marriage to my husband was a main point of stress. My family rarely visits me. They have visited three times in twelve years. The first five years they only made problems with me and refused to visit.

❖I knew I was in for major changes and disappointments. My family was number one. But to this day, I am not welcomed in their home. I went to visit them last September, and not only did they give me a hard time but refused to meet or allow my husband in their home. In fact, we were told to get going before the neighbors saw us in front of their house. That was the first time I had seen them for years.

❖Since I became Muslim I have unfortunately lost contact with many family members. This bothers me, but it has been their choice. Little by little, things are improving, however. During the past few months, several family members have contacted me, so there's hope. My father's main objection—because it's the most visible aspect of my beliefs—is wearing the hijab. He doesn't understand or approve of it. My family does not, as a general rule, know much about Islam nor do they care to know.

❖At first my parents were mad. This was because they did not understand Islam. When I started wearing hijab one and a half years after becoming a Muslim, the real trouble began. My sister still thinks I am weird and crazy and does not have much to do with me.

❖I feel distant from my family. I was very close to my brother and sisters, but now we are not as close. Religion is a very touchy subject even though I have convinced them to a certain extent that what we were following as Catholics was not all right. I feel very distant from my parents. My mother doesn't want to believe that the book (the Bible) she has been following has been changed or that Islam is the right way. She doesn't understand why I cover and don't eat food with pork by-products.

I've never opened the subject with my father. He's not very educated and he's "stuck in his ways." I really want to talk to him about it, but I don't know how or even what to say.

Most of my family think I became a Muslim for my husband's sake. They just don't understand that I truly believe in Islam with all my heart, so much that I want to preach to them the truth about Islam until they say they believe it and take shahada.

❖I know they think my husband forced me into Islam and they refuse to believe otherwise. I hoped that my mom could accept me as I am, and accept the fact that it was and is still my choice. I made the best decision of my life in choosing Islam! They refuse to acknowledge that we even believe in God, and therefore, believe we are going to hell! I hate their stubbornness!

My mother does not respect my husband's opinion on anything and won't ask him his opinion. When he tries to talk to Mom about Christianity, to get things out in the open, she refuses to talk about it; she will not even consider our point of view. My husband is very aggressive and demanding when he talks/debates with someone, but he wants so badly for her to see our side of it; he doesn't want to give up even if it regresses into a shouting match. But Mom is not used to people standing up to her. Certainly not me! My husband does not understand how something so obvious and clear to him isn't the same to someone else.

❖They really didn't comment on my marrying a Muslim a whole lot. When we first got married, some of my extended family objected—especially my grandfather—not because he was Muslim but because he wasn't American. He didn't want one of those "damn foreigners" in the family. He didn't talk to me for a couple of months. But his wife got on his case and told him it wasn't the right thing to do, to either let go of it and leave things as they were or he might lose me in the process. One time a cousin suggested that maybe my husband would convert to Christianity.

We are not a close family in that we discuss things. It tends to be mostly surface talk. One time my brother five years younger than me was asking my husband about the beliefs of the Muslims. But my dad soon let him know that was not to be discussed, so early on it was made clear that religion was not a topic to be discussed. I told my husband that I wished it was not like this, but there isn't a lot of emotional attachment.

❖My parents had to accept my change. I wasn't going to go back to Christianity or Americanism just for them. They are not open-minded, but I do my best to maintain and encourage contact, in whatever way we can afford.

I hope my parents, and all non-Muslims, will find Islam. I also accept the fact that individuals are responsible for their own actions and I will have to testify according thereto.

I don't try to push my family, or anyone into anything. If they bother me, which is often, I just pray about it and try not to let it "eat on me."

❖There are still areas left behind that cause me grief and loss which are not feeling or getting close to my mother, sisters and friends; also being close to my grandmother who tries so hard to understand and accept me and my lifestyle but hasn't gotten it yet.

❖I have not worked it out with my parents. It has been almost three years this November since they have seen us, and they still want nothing to do with any of us. My brother has done the same. My aunt talks to me, but she says things like my belief is of the devil. I don't have to worry about the holidays with my family because for nearly three years I haven't had a relationship with them.

❖My decision to convert to Islam brought mixed results from my family. My father and stepmother (my mother is deceased) totally rejected me because of it. We did not speak for more than five years. My grandparents have always made me feel welcome, but they make no bones about the fact that they totally disagree with what I'm doing.

These women might not have had the support of their families in whatever situation they chose for themselves, but certainly they have to be strong to make it without the support of their families of origin. There may well be movement in the relationship as the years go by. Family crisis, change of heart, or overwhelming need are but a few motivators for reconsidering the relationship.

Acceptance Not a Family Issue

The view expressed by two women converts was that their families of origin didn't have any say about their choice. They felt it really was not any of their family's business and if the daughter's decision was disturbing, it was the family's problem, not the daughter's.

❖The effect on my family members is nonexistent. I am an adult, and I choose to do what I want. We conduct ourselves as adults and do not ask for permission to live our lives. Religion is not an outward part of my parents' lives, and we do not talk about religious matters unless asked. When we move overseas, I hope they will understand, but if they don't, that is an issue that they will have to deal with.

❖Becoming Muslim has no effect on my relationship with my family. They knew they could accept or reject my religion; either way they had no influence. My husband (non-Muslim) accepted my changes because he respects me as a person.
    I live in the West [of the United States] and my relatives live in the East/Midwest. I feel as though they

will never fully understand. But after they found out I was a Muslim, and since there was no one that influenced me to make the choice, they accepted that Allah (SWT) guides who Allah wills.

In no instance did the questionnaire responses reflect that the women were becoming Muslim in order to anger their parents or family of origin or to try to get back at them in any way. Most were cognizant that relationships would be strained by their actions and tried to find ways to soften the news of their conversion. But for the women, this newfound faith was worth even the loss of their families if that was the only way it could be. They had chosen their path, and they intended to walk it.

5. Journeying the Muslim Path
Living and Practicing Islamic Principles

I thought the ache and hurt of that Thanksgiving weekend encounter would never pass, but we were all determined to work it through. The next time Jodi came to visit, we spent time sewing together. That was something we had loved to do from the time she was little. As we sewed, we talked. There was so much for me to learn about what Jodi had chosen.

"Mom, I brought you some tapes to listen to so you will understand more about what Islam is all about. Really, Mom, there is a lot in common with Christianity. I feel more like I can live as you raised me to live than I did before."

Yes, she probably was right about that part since our church had some expectations that were difficult for youth to live up to in society. But Islam similar to Christianity? Well, that would be hard to prove to me. It all had caused so much trouble politically and had such strange ideas. However, I was open to learning. What other choice did I have if I wanted a relationship with my daughter?

It took almost a year and a half to accept and support Jodi in the life she had chosen. I saw her so disciplined in her religion, so wanting to serve God and others around her, so strong as she wore the strange clothing with head cover to classes on the campus. And yet, she was still our Jodi who loved us, who loved to talk and be with people, who struggled to keep up with her studies, who wanted to be a nurse—and was doing it.

My friends helped me by their acceptance. I found that just sitting and crying after reading a poem or article or being in Jodi's old room was healing. I placed her in God's hands as I prayed, and no doubt there were many praying for me. I also had to help other members of the family who felt rejected. But the healing was taking place. We were a family who didn't like conflict; we wanted to love and to be accepting. We also wanted to be open to the world around us, so we began to learn about what our daughter had embraced.

❖ ❖ ❖

Jihad is a word that has become familiar to many non–Muslims because the media has often associated it with terrorist activities. Dr. Jamilah Kolocotronis, an American–born convert to Islam, in her doctoral dissertation, explored this Islamic concept, which came out of the Arabic language, meaning struggle or exertion. In the time of Muhammad, it took on new meaning as this young new religion began its growth. In her book, *Islamic Jihad: An Historical Perspective*, Dr. Kolocotronis states:

Now it took on the meaning of "struggle in the cause of Allah." After the period of Muhammad, historians began to translate jihad as "holy war," but this definition does not account for the full meaning of the term. Jihad should always be defined as struggle in the "Cause of Allah," for this definition alone encompasses all the nuances of the term.[1]

In this sense, any activity related to Islamic practice may be a struggle such as waking up for the dawn prayer if one is not an early riser. Negative connotations of jihad have developed for Westerners as radical groups (representing a small minority of people) have used the term extensively.

During the time of Muhammad, this term was applied individually, especially in the first few years as Muslim converts joined the small movement and struggled to leave the old traditions and way of life and, in spite of family members and other difficulties, take on what they had come to believe. Their personal existence was jihad as they struggled in the cause of Allah. American women who have chosen Islam are in that struggle themselves as they leave old traditions and live out their new beliefs.

Islam is an unknown to most of us. Even though we may have read a book on Islam or Muslims, studied it in a class at church, or had a unit on it at school, the content didn't have much meaning or really stay with us. Now, however, there is a walking, talking loved one who has become Muslim. Now we need to find out about that which is so important to her, to understand the journey she is on.

Islam is the name of the religion. It is an Arabic word that means "acceptance of God as Supreme" and calls for submission to the One God. The literal meaning of the word is peace—to live in peace with the Creator, within one's self, and with other people.

The followers of Islam are called Muslim. They do not like to be referred to as Muhammadans or Islamites or Islams. The people are called Muslims.

Muslims believe that Muhammad was chosen by God to be a prophet to receive God's message from the angel Gabriel. This was in Mecca in the Arabian Peninsula in the seventh century. The Qur'an (or Koran) is the book of the divine messages that came through Muhammad over a period of twenty–three years. Muslims believe that the Qur'an contains the literal and final word of God to the world.

In review, the religion is Islam, the people are Muslims, the prophet is Muhammad, and their sacred book of God's revelations through Muhammad is the Qur'an.

Articles of Faith

Three fundamental beliefs are the basis of the Islamic faith: the oneness of God, prophethood, and life after death.

The oneness of God is the foundation of their faith. Allah is the one and only God. The word Allah literally means "The God" and has no masculine, feminine, or plural form; thus Allah is elevated to the highest being. Allah is the creator of all human beings. The Muslims believe that Allah is the God of the Christians, Jews, Muslims, and others. To put anything or anyone as equal to Allah is considered blasphemous. This Unity of Allah is called tawhid, and establishes the oneness of God. Islam rejects the Christian notion of the Trinity—Father, Son, and Holy Spirit—giving no divinity to Jesus. But they do regard Jesus as a revered prophet and messenger of God.

The second article of faith is that God has provided guidance for living through such prophets as Adam, Abraham, Isaac, Jacob, Moses, Solomon, and David—some of the Old Testament prophets; John and Jesus of the New Testament; and Muhammad as the last and final prophet bringing Allah's final and literal word to humankind. As Muslims say or write each prophet's name, they say "Peace be upon him" or write (pbuh) after the name. They consider Christians, Jews, and Muslims to be people of "the book" and feel kinship through the prophets.

Prophet Muhammad is revered (not worshipped as divine) as God's messenger, and Jesus also is accepted as a messenger of God's word. Even though Muslims and Christians disagree about the divinity of Jesus, they do agree on many ideas about morality, life after death, and the day of judgment. The Qur'an teaches that adultery, murder, lying, stealing, and cheating are wrong.

Life after death is the third fundamental belief in Islam. Both belief and action are important in this life. They believe in a day of judgment in which we will be held accountable before God for our conduct. It is important that in each action there is consideration given to whether or not it is in accordance with what God has commanded.

The Five Pillars of Islam

There are five major tenets (pillars) in Islam that a Muslim is expected to follow. The first pillar is to declare shahada as the statement of conversion: "There is only one God [Allah] and Muhammad is the Messenger of God." The other four are the practical obligations of daily prayer, fasting at Ramadan, paying the annual "welfare money" to be distributed among the poor (often done in connection with Ramadan), and making the pilgrimage to Mecca.

In embracing Islam, the converts declare shahada by repeating in Arabic that they bear witness to no other deity but Allah and that Muhammad is a prophet of Allah. They also take on a way of life that has many requirements and obligations as they set their course on the "straight path." Although such practices seem to require great effort, responses to the questionnaire indicated that, overall, the women were delighted with the opportunity to have these disciplines in their lives. Some of the women respondents found fasting to be easy while others found it extremely difficult at first. Many of the women were able to slip regularly into the schedule of the five obligatory prayers each day while others had to work hard at getting into that routine. Wearing the scarf was a blessing and no problem for some; others took years to get to the point of wearing a scarf at all the required times.

The women received help in finding how to live an Islamic lifestyle from several sources. Their husbands were a strong support. They taught and directed their wives in the practice of Islam, and in the process reestablished their own faith practice. Books, videos, and audiotapes explained techniques on how to do things. Many found help from other Muslim women who were either American–born converts or were women born into Islam.

❖Since I was introduced to Islam by my husband, it was easier for me to learn to live as Muslim by observing his daily example and that of some of his friends. As for specific religious practices, he tried to teach me to pray and explained how to fast and perform ablutions, but it was my sister–in–law, who became like a sister to me during our stay in Morocco and who had just started wearing hijab a few months earlier, who helped me perfect my worship and gave me the confidence and enthusiasm to begin praying five times a day.

The first time I fasted, I was so afraid I wouldn't be able to bear it, never having gone even a short time without food. My husband explained the importance and significance of fasting, but said I didn't have to if I absolutely couldn't stand it, since Allah never requires more of us than we can bear. His moderation helped me through it, and since then I have always fasted whenever required.

The five daily prayers are probably the most difficult, since our American lifestyle often doesn't allow for them to be performed at their proper times. Sometimes time gets the best of me, but I never stop praying, even if I miss some [of the prayer times]. It may not seem like much, but the small act of prayer is what keeps Allah in my heart and mind at all times.

In each instance the women surveyed expressed the blessings and peace and satisfaction brought to their lives by the discipline required to change their lives, to focus their actions and will toward Allah.

The second of the Five Pillars of Islam is the performance of the five daily prayers (salat) that are required of all Muslims. These prayers are repeated in Arabic and have certain movements and positions for various parts. The prayers must be preceded by ablution or cleansing oneself (wudu) with water by washing of the hands up to the wrist, washing the face and head, and washing the feet up to the ankle. Women wear a special prayer covering. The person must face in a predetermined direction (toward Mecca), which symbolizes Muslim unity.

There is a prescribed schedule for when to offer these obligatory prayers: early morning before sunrise, at noon or shortly thereafter, in the late afternoon, after sunset, and about an hour later. The prayers last about five minutes each. Women are not required to pray when they are menstruating. Muslims are free, of course, to offer their own personal prayers at any time and any place and encouraged to combine them with the obligatory prayer times. Muslims almost universally leave their shoes at the door as they enter a home or mosque in order to keep the rugs clean for prayer.

❖Praying five times a day was a big commitment for me. When my husband told me a few minutes after I converted that I had to pray, I was very hesitant to do it. I wasn't used to being actively involved in my religion. But once I started, I didn't want to stop.

❖The change to Islam has helped me be more grounded, more relaxed, more focused. You can't stray too far when the next prayer pulls you back. It has certainly had a positive effect on our marriage and family life, and helped me to be a better and calmer mate and mother.

The most meaningful part of Islam for me is the internal process—the prayers and the other reading and spiritual work that is ongoing in my own life for my own spiritual development. Being able to stop a few seconds and surrender everything that is going on to Allah for guidance is a major blessing.

❖Praying according to salat (ritual prayer) times is the hardest. I'm still not in tune to clocks.

❖Learning the formal ceremony of the ritual cleansing (wudu) and the prayer itself was easy. My husband wrote the words of the prayer on a sheet of paper and added a sketch showing the movements of standing, bowing, and prostrating. I memorized the words of the prayer in just one day, but it took perhaps a week of practice to make sure that I was performing the movements correctly at the right time. I enjoyed the ritual cleansing, putting on my prayer garments, and performing the prayers because I felt I was coming closer to my Creator. I wanted to display my devotion and thankfulness for all that he had given me.

The prayers are recited in Arabic and everyone is encouraged to learn Arabic so they can read the Qur'an in the original text. Children in Islamic schools are taught Arabic.

❖I am still learning to live as a Muslim. I ask a lot of questions and read. My mother–in–law sent me a book on prayer, and I memorized the Arabic by myself. Wearing the head cover and [learning] rituals concerning prayer and clean/unclean have been hard. I watched a lot of Islamic videos and took extensive notes and attended debates.

❖The hardest part is praying. I do it phonetically in Arabic, and I'm afraid I'm pronouncing it wrong and that my prayers won't be accepted as a result. But I know that as long as I try and have good intentions, God will understand. Praying in Arabic and not knowing the Qur'an and hadith [an authoritative source of Islamic practice] like I should have been the hardest parts for me.

❖I learned to live as a Muslim mostly through my own reading and research. My husband wrote out the prayers for me in Arabic—which I read—after I had learned them in English. I am just beginning to learn sections of the Qur'an in Arabic—I can't read the fancy calligraphy of

Arabic, so I have to rely on having them read and said to me. I regard myself as still studying basic Islam.

It has been quite difficult, actually, incorporating all the religious practices I feel are important, but quite satisfying once I have managed it.

The third pillar of Islam is fasting (siyam) and is observed for the month of Ramadan, the name of the ninth month in the lunar year of the Muslim calendar. It is a sacred month for Muslims and combines fasting, prayer, and charity.

Fasting during the month of Ramadan is a religious obligation. During this time a Muslim can eat food before daybreak but is to remain without food or water or intimate sexual activities from dawn to sunset each day during the entire month. Exceptions to required fasting would be for children, the elderly, the sick, travelers, pregnant women, women who have difficulty with breast feeding, and women in menstruation. Adults should make up their missed fasts at another time after Ramadan when their situation is better. Often the breaking of the fast at sunset is done in community with other Muslims.

The last day of the fast is called Eid al–Fitr and is a major celebration time with gifts, special foods, sending of cards, and worship. The women come to love Ramadan even though the discipline of fasting is difficult at first. It is also a time when community bonds with other Muslims are strengthened as well as a time for individual spiritual growth. Sometimes there is frustration in practicing it in non–Muslim countries.

❖My first Ramadan was one to remember. It was just shy of six months after my shahada. It was easier than I thought it would be—although it was still a struggle. To be honest I broke my fast three times early in the day, my first Ramadan. It is something that takes total religious commitment and a sound mind.

❖Fasting once a year for a whole month was difficult at first, but the more I learned about why we fasted and what it did for us, the easier it became.

❖Fasting during the holy month of Ramadan was the hardest practice I have encountered. Before my first fast, I was worried that I would not be able to do it and that I would fail this challenge. Of course I was able to do it because fasting is easy when you are doing it for God.

A few times my throat was extremely dry or I had a headache and wanted to take medication, but I abstained. I thought about Imam Husain (pbuh) and his followers (peace be upon them) who were martyred thirsty in the desert of Karbala. I thought about the homeless and poverty–stricken people who did not know when or if they will have another meal.

Fasting helps one gain nearness to God, spiritual awareness, kindness and generosity for others, humility, and thankfulness. Because it is such a spiritual time, I look forward to the holy month of Ramadan each year. During the last ten days of Ramadan I feel sad that it will be over so soon.

❖Living as a Muslim has not been that difficult because I have unconsciously been doing that for a number of years. My husband does help make living as a Muslim easier because he is Muslim as well and it's easier to do something when you have company. The only times I find religious practices difficult is around Christmas time when *everything* is Christianized, and I have to explain why I don't celebrate. The other time is during Ramadan when people ask what I want for lunch and I tell them I am fasting. It's difficult for people to understand, and I know that they judge me for it, but I will not compromise my beliefs for a sandwich from a fast–food restaurant.

The fourth pillar of Islam is the paying of a charity tax or tithing called zakat, and it is to be paid during Ramadan along with the fasting and worship.

The fifth and last pillar of Islam is hajj, a pilgrimage to Mecca for those who have the financial means. Opportunity for the pilgrimage occurs once each year and is the largest gathering of people in the world as 2 to 2 1/2 million gather from every continent of the globe to fulfill this obligation.

The Muslim Lifestyle in American Society

Islam addresses all aspects of life including personal morality, politics, and commerce; Islam is a way of life. Very important is the concept of ummah, the community in which God's will is attainable only through a society built around Islamic principles. Much time and discussion is spent on interpreting in action the prescribed manner of living. The women learn quickly what it is they are expected to do and make decisions of how they will implement those expectations in their lives.

The extreme change in dress is probably the hardest shift for the parents and relatives to accept when a daughter becomes Muslim. It seems to us such an extreme statement about what they have chosen. For some of the women themselves, choosing to dress modestly and cover themselves has been readily accepted and incorporated in their practice; for others it has been very difficult to do.

The passage from the Qur'an that prescribes the covering describes it this way:

Tell the believing men to lower their gaze, and protect their private parts. That is purer for them. Verily, Allah is All–Aware of what they do. And tell the believing women to lower their gaze, and protect their private parts and not to show off their adornment except only that which is apparent and to draw their veils over their bosoms and not to display their adornment except to their husbands, or their fathers, or their husband's fathers, or their sons, or their husband's sons, or their brothers, or their brothers' sons, or their sisters' sons, or their wives, or the slaves whom their right hands possess, or male servants free of physical needs, or small children who have no sense of the shame of sex. And let them not stamp their feet so as to reveal what they hide of their adornment. And beg Allah to forgive you all, O believers, that you may be successful."—S24, A30–31

Various Islamic countries have traditions on how to wear the cover. The basic tradition is loose–fitting clothes (not "see through" or defining the figure) which cover all but the face and hands. In some countries the veil over the face is worn also. Some wear flowery bright colors or beads and fringe; others wear only the more serious plain colors such as white, beige, brown, green, blue, black, or soft prints. Those in the know are often able to tell what country a woman is from by the way she covers. Not all women who are Muslim cover their hair with a scarf, but most do try to dress modestly.

❖Wearing hijab was easy, but people were always asking me if I had some sort of disease. They seemed to assume that I had lost my hair and I was covering up my baldness. Then after I explained about the religious reasons and significance of wearing hijab, they would say, "You mean I can never see your beautiful hair again?" It was as if my personal choice of practicing my own religion was taking away one of their pleasures or privileges and they did not approve of that! They missed the point.

❖I have worked out with my parents and other family members my choice to be Muslim. The main point of stress has been hijab or the Islamic dress. I think this is a constant reminder and embarrassment for them. If I were

Muslim but did not cover, I think they could accept it more readily. My hope is that they will understand Islam and like it on their own, not just because of me.

✦Taking on Islamic religious practices wasn't hard once I did it for a while. Wearing hijab was the one that took the most getting used to, both for me and for others around me. I lived in a very small town and I got strange looks there, and several people asked me about it. But in our larger university town, the majority of people are educated about it and see women wearing hijab around town. I started wearing hijab in winter, so it wasn't difficult until summertime. Many people wear a scarf or hat in winter, but when summer came and I was still wearing a scarf, I did stand out in a crowd. But Islam is not about blending in or "when in America, do as the Americans do." It is about standing up for what you believe and what you know is right, even if others do not, whether Muslim or non–Muslim.

✦It has been easy for me to take on the religious prac-tices. I had no trouble accepting and enjoying the benefits of praying, fasting, giving up alcohol. My biggest battle is the head covering, the scarf. Nobody knows this though, since I accept and submit to the covering for modesty reasons.

✦Six months after shahada, I observed my first Ramadan. I had been contemplating the issue of hijab, but was too scared to take that step before. I had already begun to dress more modestly, and usually wore a scarf over my shoulders. When I visited [a Muslim] sister, she told me, "All you have to do is move that scarf from your shoulders to your head, and you'll be Islamically dressed." At first I didn't feel ready to wear hijab because I didn't feel strong enough in my faith. I understood the reason for it, agreed with it, and admired the women who did wear it. They looked so pious and noble. But I knew that if I wore it, people would ask me a lot of questions, and I didn't feel ready or strong enough to deal with that.

This changed as Ramadan approached, and on the first day of Ramadan, I woke up and went to class in hijab. Alhamdulillah, I haven't taken it off since. Something about Ramadan helped me to feel strong and proud to be a Muslim. I felt ready to answer anybody's questions.

❖Covering was a very gradual change. I went from jeans to skirts and long sleeve shirts or blazers. Then I decided I would wear the scarf and long clothes or coat after I had my first child. It was very hard to cope with the looks and questions about the way I dressed (i.e., long sleeves and jackets in the summertime) while I was working. That's why I waited to fully cover. Once I did start fully covering I was very uncomfortable and felt so different from everyone else that I almost took it off, as if to prove to everyone (even those I didn't know) that I was still the same person as before. But I kept it on and eventually got used to it. Now I get mad at people who stare at me or make fun of me, but that only makes me want to wear it more. I've been covering for three years.

Featured throughout an entire issue of *Islamic Sisters International* (January 1994) was the topic, "Hijab—Definition and Discrimination."[2] Many of the women described the discrimination that occurred in the workplace when interviewing for jobs. Some had difficulty dealing with the jeers and name–calling experienced in various public places. One stated that she feels the non–Muslim women are more offended by the head cover than the non–Muslim men. In these articles the women encouraged covering as very necessary and in some cases the word "obligation" was used.

The editor of the magazine encouraged all sisters to actively participate to end discrimination from unfair business practices to exclude, deny, or otherwise hide those sisters who cover, and work for the rights they are guaranteed while living in the United States or Canada. A date was set and the sisters were encouraged to wear halal Islamic clothing to their places of work or regular activities, to write or call their senator, to call or write local and national news to protest unfair misrepresentation, and to arrange peaceful picket lines in appropriate places.

The women wearing hijab express not only what a meaningful experience it is for them but also the frustration they sometimes have. Many women converts are choosing to wear the cover in this Western setting, are establishing Muslim homes, and are concerned that the rights extended to them as women in the Islamic faith are actualized in their lives. Some of their stories in regard to these areas are included here.

❖The best Islamic right by far is the hijab. I have a right to be looked at as a moral woman, not a piece of meat to be gawked at. People look at my eyes when talking to me. I am treated like a lady as a general rule. There are always those who jump at a chance to condemn. I would be more encouraged to go into the work force if it weren't for those few people ignorant of Islam.

❖We live in a very strong and close–knit Muslim community. I graduated magna cum laude last year with a degree in child development. I have had several jobs, from secretary to preschool teacher, with no problems about my hijab. I'm active in the community and still do volunteer work.

❖Due to hijab, there are a lot of prejudices out there. I definitely can't hold a very public "meeting people" job.

❖The only obstacles that have been placed in my way as a Muslim woman have not been from Muslims or Islam, but from the society in which we live. One often feels like a fish swimming upstream in America, like constantly explaining hijab. I have been denied jobs because of my hijab and have been otherwise openly discriminated against. Nonetheless, I am truly grateful for hijab. It is liberating in a sense that pro–ERA women will never know. I feel honored to represent Islam in such a powerful way as to be recognized as Muslim whenever I venture out.

❖My perception of being a woman has changed. I no longer find freedom in tight pants and miniskirts, but through hijab and modesty. I no longer believe men and women have to be the same to be equal and that there are roles each are better suited for. At the same time, we all (men and women) have our own unique, individual talents and need to have the opportunity to nourish them.

❖ I wish non–Muslims understood that hijab is only a small part of being a Muslim woman. It is too bad that the majority tend to "judge the book (or woman) by the cover(ing)"—meaning they measure Islam by a style of dress. In a society which claims to envision a "freer" means of life for women, the American male attitude toward women actually puts women way down by promoting the sex–symbol image. Hijab removes the possibilities for men to "ogle" and demands they view women as people rather than objects.

Only one woman in the survey indicated that she wears the veil, covering everything but the eyes. At present she lives in a Muslim country, but did veil in the United States prior to moving.

❖I cover from head to toe—gloves, socks, the whole package. I wear a hair cover under a cloak, and I wear a veil. I anticipated so many problems, yet I can hardly believe how easy it has been. I even veiled for 3 1/2 years in the United States with no trouble. So many people learned about Islam because they were curious about the veil. It is a bit hot, but when the temperature gets over 100 degrees everything is hot to wear! I greatly prefer this dress to anything. Especially people who understand the reason for the veil and dress have been supportive and respectful. I get special treatment everywhere I go here and in the States. Old Muslim ladies will do anything for me. I get great seats on planes, people let me in front of them in lines, and sometimes merchants here in this country will give me free gifts or free service.

Dawah is the word used in place of the Christian terms "witnessing" or "evangelism." The scarf is often an opportunity for a woman to tell about Islam because she is more apt to be questioned than a man. As one woman wrote, "You can see us coming a mile away but [an observer] can't really tell if a man is a Muslim or not."

❖I have learned and am still learning to put into practice what is allowed and forbidden. It was difficult to get used to covering, but now I am proud to be a Muslim and I find dawah, at the proper times, is my passageway. I just have to ignore the prejudices or use them as even more of a reason to put my beliefs into practice.

In addition to dress, acceptable social behaviors are encouraged that reflect the Islamic culture as interpreted by tradition in various Muslim countries and influenced by family and personal preferences. In general, modesty in behavior as well as in dress is important between men and women. Men and women should be modest in their conversations with one another, being cautious to avoid flirtations and personal innuendoes. Men and women who are not related according to the previous Qur'anic passage attempt to avoid being alone with one another.

When they become Muslim, many of the women choose to stay home rather than be employed, especially if they have children. Others are still in the work force or attending universities. Each woman has to gain a "sense" of how she will present herself as a Muslim woman in her situation.

❖One of the major changes I made was to be careful how I talked to men. I needed to do it more maturely—not talk about personal things.

❖I cannot greet my male friends as I used to or even stop for an impromptu talk. My husband's co–workers and friends are off–limits for even a chat by the car while I'm waiting for him to come out of work.

❖The religious practices are not hard, but some of the Western ideas are hard to break and can pull you from religious duties. For example, a Muslim should not be rude, but polite and firm in belief. I find it hard to be a good Muslim when I want to tell people (who are rude) to get lost. Also Western TV can be contradictory to Islamic values. This is the hardest for me.

❖During my first Ramadan, we gathered together and the shaikh [elder or spiritual leader] would give talks. These talks were so pure and meaningful that they stood in stark contrast to the ugliness I found happening among the people. And this is a reality I find limiting our Islamic practice: How come it is so difficult for people to really practice and live up to the model of Prophet Muhammad (pbuh)? Maybe I have to realize that Americans' morals have already so much deteriorated. It is possible I need to thank my parents for such a solid and basic upbringing, where corruption and jealousy, anger and hatred, impatience and other human ugliness weren't present.

❖When I became Muslim, I had guidelines to express the beliefs I already had. Yet these changes were tough. It was hard to excuse myself from class or work to pray. When my clothing changed (covering my hair) I lost a lot of friends. I also had to explain to male friends that it was no longer appropriate for me to see them. I've also been shunned by a lot of relatives who tell my family I'll burn in hell!

I became cleaner and quieter the further I went into the religion. I became highly disciplined. I had not intended to marry before I was Muslim, yet I quickly became a wife, then a mother!

Islam has provided a framework that has allowed me to express the beliefs I already had such as modesty, kindness, love. It also led me to happiness through marriage and the births of two children. Before Islam, I had no desire to have my own family since I hated kids!

No matter how bad things get, I have something I can hang on to. Never do I feel alone or desperate because I know Allah is close, and I know he is testing me to make me stronger. The sisterhood and brotherhood of Muslims has been a comfort to me in hard times.

The role of the women in the home is of utmost importance in Islam, and the emphasis on the rearing of children and the care of the home is taken very seriously by Muslim women. Often the children are home schooled by the mothers. Some of the parents of Muslim women converts are upset when their daughters choose to stay home. They are afraid it might be an indication of the woman not having an opportunity to reach her full potential. This concern is especially strong if the parents have paid for their daughter's education.

After marrying a Muslim (or even after becoming acquaintanced with a Muslim), a woman learns quickly not to serve pork or anything that contains pork products to a Muslim. Often by the time the women convert, they have decided to eat only "halal" meats and foods. Halal means "slaughtered according to Islamic law." This takes a lot of dedication on the part of the couple because halal meats are not readily available unless they live in a heavily populated Muslim community, and the meats are usually more expensive. The women often learn to cook many of the foods that their husbands appreciate from their own heritage.

❖To follow the Qur'anic injunction of eating only Muslim slaughtered–approved meats was easy. I knew the Bible prohibited eating pork and wondered why Christians did not follow that law. Eating meat that my husband slaughtered according to Islamic law gave me a sense of pride that he was following God's ordinance and that God was pleased with us. We shared our meat with other Muslims, and I was glad that we had the opportunity to help them obey God's law.

❖A point of stress in visiting my family is our commitment to eating only Muslim slaughtered halal meats. We are reluctant to eat anything, so we bring our own food. Even though we explained the Islamic method of slaughter, they were uncomfortable with us bringing our own food. They thought this was another rejection, as if their food was not good enough for us or was unclean. However, when they come to visit in our home, they eat whatever I cook, and we seem to have a much happier and less stressful time.

These are just a few of the many changes women converts make as they develop and grow in their faith journey as a Muslim. They seem to help and support each other through the initial journey. Although the basic Islamic precepts are shared by all Muslim sects, there are some differences in how people choose to fit these practices into their daily lives. The extent to which they choose to follow and interpret these precepts differs from person to person and culture to culture.

❖Living in Egypt and Saudi Arabia has influenced me greatly, and has resulted in my really knowing that the manifestation of Islam varies from place to place, but the most important thing is the way we personally live out the religion and to make sure we always approach it with good intentions.

Muslims feel it is important to do the "right thing" as far as they can determine what that is. They view the religion of Islam as a comprehensive system dealing with every facet of life including the life of the individual, the society, and the government. The women have turned to many sources of information in order to better understand the system of beliefs they have chosen to represent. The women do not seem to have followed blindly, but they have spent time learning and seeking out answers in order to practice more knowledgeably.

❖I learned to live as a Muslim both through books and the help of other Muslims. Good books describe the things that can and can't be eaten, how one should dress, the things one should not have in one's house, etc. A new Muslim has to get this information through books and other Muslims because it takes a lot of time to learn all of it from the Qur'an and hadis. I did study the Qur'an and hadis; I didn't just take things blindly. If someone told me something, sometimes I wanted to look it up to see for myself if I would make that same conclusion after reading about it.

❖My Saudi friend was the one who taught me how to live as a Muslim. She showed me how to pray, how to make wudu (cleansing or ablution), and how to socialize with other Muslims. She answered every Islamic question I had, from marriage and children to hadith and fiqh (science of Islamic law). I obtained (through the Saudi embassy) an English–Arabic version of the Holy Qur'an as well as books on a variety of Islamic subjects. Islam as a lifestyle was easy for me to adopt because my previous lifestyle was not very extravagant. The Arabic language was probably the most difficult thing for me. Praying, fasting, wearing hijab, etc., all came easy for me.

❖I really did not have to learn to live as a Muslim because I already had the lifestyle of a Muslim. I dressed morally, I did not eat pork, I did not drink, and I tried to do right by my fellow human beings. To be quite honest, no one had to help me to be a Muslim. I learned on my own. The only things I had to change were my holidays and worship day. This was quite easy for me because when I converted to Islam it was a way of life for me. In fact, I enjoy the fact that Islam makes it simple to be a practicing Muslim.

❖I learned to live as a Muslim from other Muslims. I was blessed to meet two very knowledgeable couples who taught both my husband and me the things that every Muslim needs to know. Although many things in Islam are not complicated, living in a non–Islamic society makes them seem as such. I also feel that it depends on what area of the country one lives. In most of the larger cities, especially in the North, there are large Muslim communities. This makes it a bit easier to find items such as halal meats. Also the non–Muslims are familiar with Muslim dress and some Islamic practices; therefore, they seem to be more tolerant and less awestruck by our presence. I find that having close ties with other Muslim families makes it easier to deal with the difficulties.

Rights of Muslim Women

The Arabia of the seventh century was a setting in which the killing of baby daughters was common and women had few rights and were often mistreated. The Qur'an gave women the rights to hold title to property, to receive inheritance, to receive a dowry, to have a say in whom she chooses to marry, to be supported and protected by her husband, and other rights too numerous to list.

Dr. Riffat Hassan, a woman and Muslim theologian at the University of Louisville states, "I remember how stricken I felt when I first began to see the glaring discrepancy between Islamic ideals and Muslim practice insofar as women are concerned."[3] She believes women in other countries are largely unaware of the differences, for despite the important roles played by the wives of Muhammad, "the Islamic tradition has remained rigidly patriarchal . . . prohibiting the growth of scholarship among women particularly in the realm of religious thought. . . ."[4] Thus it follows that Muslim women have not been cognizant of how their human "rights have been violated by their male–dominated and male–centered society . . . [unaware] that Islam has given women more rights than any other religious tradition."[5]

American–born women who have converted to Islam also have the challenge of feminist leadership as they interpret the rights that have been extended to women through the Qur'an. American women who have not been exposed to an Islamic culture have a unique opportunity to see the rights of women

Islamically interpreted and practiced in the American setting. These ideas are affecting and, hopefully, changing incorrect customs which have developed in Muslim societies. The women suggest both frustration and gratefulness for such customs in the Muslim community, the ummah.

❖Sometimes I feel Muslim women aren't given a chance to speak out about their opinions or views on things within the Muslim community. They are put in the back and hidden away. If I go to a lecture not in a masjid, I like to sit near the front, so I can see and hear the speaker. I am dressed Islamically, so why should I sit in the back just because someone thinks men cannot control themselves? Men need to take the responsibility for their own actions. Women cannot always be hidden so men won't think bad thoughts. We should dress and act so as not to promote that, but I still will not live my life locked up in a cage, or in the back row at a university lecture. I can live my life with respect and dignity, and live as a Muslim woman at the same time.

❖As a Muslim woman I would like to see women take a more active role in society—be more outspoken instead of the silent shadows Western cultures see Muslim women as. Islam gives Muslim women many rights. One of the main reasons for hijab is to enter society. Muslim women should play an active part in being role models for children.

The move to recognize the rights of Muslim women is of great concern, and these rights are treasured by Muslim women in the United States and Canada. They believe that Allah, through the Qur'an 1400 years ago, set in place rights for women that have never, at any time, been equalled in the spiritual, intellectual, political, social, and economic areas of life. Some of these rights are reflected in the following in regard to maintenance and kindly treatment, education and a career, and being regarded as an equal with man before God but with roles that are somewhat different in their responsibilities.

❖I have the same rights as other women. I have the freedom of education and career if I desire. I think actually Muslim women are treated with a lot of respect. I've been married eleven years and my husband has never shown disrespect for me or tried to take away my freedoms of opinion or choice. We have argued about them but he hasn't tried to stop them.

❖My husband has been kind and generous to me and allowed me to make decisions in our home. I clean and decorate our home as I wish. I make it a place of peacefulness and rest—a place where all family members can relax and soothe their anxieties and forget their worries of the outside world. When I wanted to leave my teacher/counselor position before our first child was born, he willingly accepted my decision to stay at home and never asked me to keep working to help pay our expenses.

❖One area I am grateful for in my position as a married woman is that I prefer to let someone else make the big decisions. My husband is the leader of my household, but as I tell my kids, I'm vice president. Also I am treated with respect as well as dignity. I like it.

❖As a Muslim woman, I have the right to worship, to choose a good husband, and to lead a clean life. I have the right to be protected and not abused. I am grateful for a husband who puts his wife first into consideration, a husband who asks for and respects my opinion. I don't feel any real disadvantages as a Muslim woman. The only thing perhaps is in regard to finding outside employment. Sometimes, it's hard to find a job (especially with non–Muslims).

❖Definitely I appreciate the right not to be hassled by men for dates, meetings, and obnoxious cliches and lines. I also am experiencing more freedom in my choices pertaining to my occupation, money I earned, and personal limitations according to *my* needs—not someone else's.

❖My becoming a Muslim gave me the courage to stand up against ignorance and to take charge of and responsibility for my life. My life as a Christian was continually filled with dilemma after dilemma in which I hoped my father or someone else would save me. My outlook on life was analogous to the faith. Unfortunately, such an immature outlook not only hinders personal growth but also affects self–esteem. Islam gave me the self–esteem to be able to make great decisions without being afraid to carry through with them.

❖A Muslima [a Muslim woman] is not responsible for her support at all. The husband has to totally shoulder her support, including clothing and Islamic learning materials. Any money she gets, either child support from previous marriage, working, her mahar [dowry], her inheritance, or anything like that is hers to save or spend as she sees fit (as long as it falls under Islamic guidelines for halal). Her husband cannot touch any of it! If she is working, she can contribute to the household if she chooses, because she is taking time away from the house to work. The rest is hers and hers alone. My husband didn't realize this when we got married. When I explained it to him, he said that men sure got the short end of the stick! That is true! If I get a few dollars from somewhere, I can spend it on a new dress, or jewelry, or save it; but my husband first has to pay all the household bills before he can spend any money on himself. Men have a lot of responsibility. I do worry about the household, but it is not my responsibility to meet the bills every month. My husband knows that it is his total responsibility.

❖The one right I have that's very important to me is not having to work and getting the chance to be with my daughter! It also is nice to have my husband provide for me at my standards and above without really asking. Nice home, clothes, the basics, and more. I feel the home is for the wife and mother, and I love it. I'm very, very grateful to have this opportunity, and it wouldn't be possible if I weren't married. There are no areas not open to me as a Muslim woman.

What They Left Behind

The journey in the Muslim path required the women to leave behind many of the things they grew up with. The women respondents didn't indicate that they felt any great sense of loss or grief for what they had left behind in converting to Islam. Most responded with statements of thanksgiving that they had found this way of living, but some admitted having to adjust to giving up something previously enjoyed.

❖I feel *no* loss or grief in the life I "left behind." I don't feel I left anything behind, only grew into what I wished to become. I don't know what I would have become, but I know I prayed for deliverance from the way I was seeing my life go and the manner of the society.

❖The hardest change was when I started eating only Islamic meat, not being able to eat the main courses at my family's dinners. At the time I converted, we had to kill our own sheep and chicken at the beginning and it was a pain.

❖There is nothing in my life before my husband or before Islam that I miss. I have always wanted a logical solution to my religious questions and the ability to research in peace. Religion is an institution of faith and obedience to the intangible, and I have found something in Islam that has touched my heart and feels as natural as breathing.

❖There are no areas that I left behind that I feel a loss or grief for. The only thing that I grieve for is my family to come to Islam.

❖I still feel grief and loss—although not as much as before—during Christmas time. I loved to sing the carols and feel the "magic." I've always been deeply committed to God (except those few years in college) and am very spiritual.

❖The only thing I miss about Christianity is decorations and giving and receiving gifts at Christmas. That's it.

❖The area that I feel a loss is being able to go swimming because I love to swim and my husband doesn't know how. I want my son to know how much fun swimming can be. Now I don't see how I can help him learn except for a stranger doing it.

❖I miss the air going through my hair because I wear hijab. But I tell myself to keep a strong faith and that Allah will reward me.

❖I can't think of anything I left behind that I miss. I was already tired of the party scene and longed to get married and have babies, just before finding Islam. I could see my previous life was headed downward. I was a bit vain, however, and it took years to adopt hijab.

❖I sure would like a bacon sandwich once in awhile!

❖What is painful to have left behind is the very close–knit and rich network of meaningful and lively friendships.

❖I wasn't really sad to leave anything behind except maybe sausage pizza, but I have since found a place in our area that serves halal beef sausage pizza.

❖I have worn hijab ever since converting. Although I recognize its protection, I have found myself wanting to run out to the grocery store without it. I miss the beach, swimming, and basking in the sun.

❖Connecting all of my life to God is the most meaningful part of Islam to me. I need and love the discipline of prayer and all required of Islam. I now *love* hijab, and I'm grateful that God saved me from where I was headed and where so many of my friends are stuck.

The woman converting to Islam takes on a whole new way of relating to the world. She is accepting a set of practices that, although they may vary with cultural interpretations, are basically universal. She has the task of blending her Western upbringing with that of her husband's culture, that of the Islamic practices, and that of the ummah that is her support group. All this she must do plus rebuilding relationships with her family of origin.

The woman converting to Islam will have the responsibility to help interpret the rights extended to Muslim women in the settings in which they are, whether moving to countries with majority Muslim population or associating with new converts or immigrants to America. They will serve as mentors to teach new converts and to extend friendship to new Muslim immigrants. For American-born converts, jihad becomes a personal reality as they struggle to live out their commitment to God by living and practicing Islamic principles.

Notes

1. Jamilah Kolocotronis, *Islamic Jihad: An Historical Perspective* (Indianapolis: American Trust Publications, 1990), x.

2. *Islamic Sisters International,* vol. 2, no. 7 (January 1994).

3. Riffat Hassan, "The Issue of Woman–Man Equality in the Islamic Tradition," in *Women's and Men's Liberation —Testimonies of Spirit,* ed. Leonard Grob, Riffat Hassan, and Haim Gordon (New York: Greenwood Press, 1991), 68.

4. Ibid., 66.

5. Ibid., 66.

6. Accepting the Daughter's Journey
Reconciling the Lifestyle Choices Between Daughter and Parents

It had been three years since Jodi told us of her conversion to Islam. The editor of our church magazine was looking for articles on reconciling relationships in the family, and I felt that I could write about what had happened as Jodi and I worked to heal our relationship. I wrote the story and sent it to Jodi to get her approval to submit it to the magazine. I generally told how devastated we were when she became Muslim and how we had worked at "working it out" in those first few years. My story closed with the following:

A basic concept I have is that God is the God of all the world, who loves all people, moves in their lives, and is basic to their expression of religion. As a result of this growing experience, I can say to my daughter: "Jodi, you will be far away from me when you go to Iran. I shall miss you, but I am thankful that during these past few years we have rebuilt our relationship. I have let go of trying to control your life choices, even though I didn't realize I was doing that. Now I support you in your decisions. I appreciate that you are strong in your faith in God, that you care for other people, and that you have committed your life to goodness. You will be a great blessing to people wherever you are.

"You can always count on me for support and love. Thank you for helping me understand that you are not rejecting us—that you have just chosen a different way to express your calling in life. Thank you for being grateful to us for giving you a firm foundation on which to build your life. Thank you for loving us. You are our daughter, our friend, our window to another part of the world. I love you." (Reprinted by permission, *Saints Herald*, 132:17, November 1985, pp. 18, 19, 24.)

The surprising part was that Jodi not only approved the article but responded by writing her side of the story and how she struggled in her choice to pit her love for her parents against her desire to follow what she had come to believe. Here is her side of the story as told at that time.

And Jodi Mohammadzadeh Responds

Before Reza and I were married, religion was at the head of many of our discussions. Despite the fact that our religions had two very different names and faces, we found that our feelings for God were much alike. Here was a man with whom I could express and explore my religious ideas and feelings. Somehow the questions he stirred in me only brought me closer to him. A feeling of trust and friendship grew between us, and we both realized that we wanted to continue to share and support each other.

Unfortunately, during the time I had been getting to know Reza, my two best friends knew very little about him. How was I going to tell my mother and father that I had found my life's partner? I needed their acceptance and approval in this, as I had needed it for most other things. I trusted these two dear people for their wisdom and wanted them to be pleased now, as I had always wanted them to be pleased with me. But they barely knew Reza, and it would require time and effort to make them as sure as I was.

When we were married, we agreed that we should study each other's religion to have a better understanding of each other's backgrounds. We hoped that this would continue to bring us together in our feelings despite the difference in the names of our faiths. We continued our learning. Reza sometimes went to church with my family and discussed religious concepts with them. I read articles and introductory books on basic Islamic concepts. Neither of us felt the need to convert the other.

Our move to Arkansas put some distance between my family and us. During this time I became increasingly interested in Islam. Reza and I began praying together, and our faith grew. My faith was not only expanding but taking shape. My interest in Islam had matured to the point where it had become part of me.

I had no idea how my parents would take this news. I did not even have a plan of how to tell them. I realized it would hurt them, but I felt confident and comfortable with my decision. I needed their approval—or at least acceptance—and for them to be as pleased as I was. They were not pleased, and they did not approve.

I am only now beginning to realize the strength that my faith provided me that weekend. There was a period when I was unsure whether I had completely broken the bonds between my parents and me or had just stretched them severely. Mom reacted verbally; I could deal with that. Looking withdrawn and deep in thought, Dad said very little. I saw it would take time for them to get over the initial shock and anger, but I did not know how long or what our relationship would be. I did know I was not willing to give up either my new faith or my love for my parents.

After that Thanksgiving, when Reza and I went back to Arkansas, I felt empty and uncertain as a result of the weekend's events. Phone calls home were bland. My dreams were filled with scenes of parental rejection, and I would awake crying hysterically. Like my parents, I felt something was being torn from me. One thought kept me from losing hope. Knowing that my parents were believers in the same God I had come to trust and love so much, I would wait for them, and let God help them heal.

Since I told my family of my conversion to Islam, our relationship has gone through many changes. No doubt it will go through many more. I can honestly say I have never loved and appreciated my parents more than I do now. I would not trade our new relationship for any other.

"Mom and Dad, thank you for trying so hard to be understanding. I will continue to look to you for your wisdom and support. As your friend, I will try to support you too. All my love"—Jodi. (Reprinted by Permission. *Saints Herald*, 132:17, November 1985, pp. 18, 19, 24.)

Reconciliation was something both of us desired. It didn't mean that Islam was something I wanted to embrace as my own, but I did learn to appreciate what it was calling my daughter and her friends to be.

❖ ❖ ❖

Change in our lives caused by choices of family members can be very destructive and cause broken relationships. We can become confused in how to relate to each other, and we become upset and frustrated. The hope in all of this is that even in our brokenness, we can experience reconciliation as we move to put the pieces of our relationship back together. The new relationship may reflect a different pattern of relating and acceptance. Reconcilation is a two–way process helping us reach out toward each other to mend our hurt and anger, to adjust to new ways of thinking, and to regain our balance.

Just as the daughters struggle to gain a sense of balance with their parents as they live out their new roles, so do the parents struggle in accepting the daughter's journey in her choice to be Muslim. The women responding to the questionnaire received Parent Questionnaires (Appendix B) that they could share with their parents if they so desired. Seven parents responded to the questionnaires, telling their stories of struggle and adjustment. Responses by both the daughters and the parents indicate that hurt occurred because of lifestyle choices by the daughter that were different from the parents.

The questionnaire for the parents asked for reactions to the conversion of their daughters to Islam. They were to rate on a scale of 1 to 10 (1 being completely devastated to 10 being really okay with it) how they first felt about the daughter's conversion to Islam, and they were to rate on a similar scale of 1 to 10 how they felt about it at the time of answering the questionnaire. From 3 to 12 years had passed from the time of the daughters' conversions to the time of completing the questionnaire.

In each case the rating had increased, indicating an improvement in their relationship. If they rated their reaction 1 or 2 at first, the later feeling was a 5 or 6. If they rated their reaction at 6 or 7 at first, they felt an 8 or 9 later. Following are three of the stories of how the parents reacted and have worked through the situation.

Story 1: Acceptance in the Face of Concern

The daughter has been a Muslim for 4 1/2 years. She was raised Catholic, but in her senior year of college, she began a search for her own religion. She quickly went through two other Christian churches. The mother, who is the narrator of this story, rated her feelings regarding the conversion as a 1 at first, but had moved to a 6 at the time of the questionnaire.

My daughter had begun talking with a Muslim man at a store near us and decided to join that faith. We knew she was studying Islam, but she kept her conversion a secret until some ladies of that faith sent her a bouquet of flowers. I've never invaded my children's privacy, but this time I decided to look at the card which read "Congratulations on becoming a Muslim." We didn't say anything to her at the time. I hoped she would confide in us. Then one day, she asked if she could bring a man to meet us. He was [from a Muslim country]. He asked our permission to date our daughter with the intention of marriage. He explained his religion wouldn't allow him to be alone with her unless they were engaged. We were both shocked as we didn't know he existed until 30 minutes before. Her father was quite up–front with him, expressing his dissatisfaction that women were treated "as inferiors" and were forced to wear that old–fashioned garb while men wore what they wanted. I was more polite, but equally shocked. I had hoped my girls would not be afraid to confide in me as I was in my mother, and I was very hurt. She had already been through two religions, and I was worried that she might marry and then find she didn't agree with this one also.

I wasn't crazy about the idea of her marrying a foreigner. They might go there to live and I had heard stories about such cases as the one portrayed in *Not Without My Daughter*. I had read something about Islam and was impressed with their devotion. I had always assumed Allah and my heavenly Father were the same. I told that to her husband [to be]. We could not withhold permission as she was twenty–five years old, and that if this man treated her okay he would suit me fine as he seemed to suit her. Really we were extremely worried about her mental condition at the time because of several other behaviors and maladjustments in her life.

She was our daughter. We loved her and wanted to continue being a part of her life. I believed that all have a right to their own relationship with God and have the right to live their own life in their own way. We argued, fussed, cried, wrote letters until we were basically satisfied. It was a very trying time for me. I felt out of control. I felt my worst fears had been realized. I went to a doctor and was put on medication for six months for nerves.

We now have a pretty good relationship. We talk, but I don't agree with a lot she says and does. Customs like wearing apparel [covering] bother me. I feel Islamic men are so afraid of their sexuality that the women have the burden of helping them control it. One of her sisters wants to kidnap her and reprogram her. One brother doesn't have much to do with her but the other does. All her siblings love her, but think she is mentally mixed up.

The main points of our stress are our differences in religion (Jesus, Muhammad) and the differing cultural values. We do not dine together because she is not able to be in the same room with male first cousins and brother –in–law. [Note: This seems an unusual cultural restriction when compared with the other stories.]

For celebrations and holidays we don't even invite our daughter because she will not acknowledge our holidays or even our birthdays. She wouldn't go to lunch with me on her birthday for fear it was a celebration. Frankly, I don't like this at all. She wouldn't even come over to have her picture made with us and all five kids because her brother–in–law was also here. I think this is a stupid rule and I think it's more cultural than religious. Her father thinks her husband should do some of the changing, and she shouldn't have to do it all. Her husband and father get into arguments.

Not being able to have friends or male relatives is difficult. We tried having separate rooms for males and females once. All the males except her husband ended up in the living room with the ladies. But I enjoy being with our daughter, and I really like her husband despite the stresses.

Really, a lot of the worries I had about her did not stem from her conversion but from what I observed of her mental state. She told us we were going to hell. We raised her in the wrong faith, and we fed her the wrong foods. So I think part of the problem stemmed from the fact she was going through a crisis of young adulthood (my opinion, not hers). She began not to trust doctors, medicine, synthetic vitamins, homogenized milk. So what we were dealing with had more to do with our reaction than her actual conversion. I felt she was afraid of sex, afraid of working, afraid of life, and was hiding behind Islam. I still think that's a strong possibility, but she seems happy and to love her husband and her way of life.

So I have to accept and hope she will be able to lead the best life she can. The hope I have for us is that we will learn to accept and respect each other more and that she and her dad will reach an understanding.

This family had to deal with a practice unique to the husband's culture, that practice being that his wife (their daughter) evidently should not be in the same room with men other than her immediate family even if she is wearing hijab. The parents are also concerned about other reactions she has had to life.

Story 2: Openness to Diversity and Change

The next family has a history of being more open to and accepting of a variety of cultural settings in which there is more give and take by members of the family. The daughter has been Muslim for seven years. The father holds a Ph.D. in counseling and is employed in a college setting. The mother is deceased and there is a stepmother. There are four adult children from the father's family and four adult children from the stepmother's family. The father, whose story follows, rated his first reaction as a 6 with the later rating as a 9.

My daughter's major in college brought her into contact with international students. From her family orientation, she had a high degree of tolerance for people from other cultures and belief systems. I was widowed, and had married a Jewish woman.

When our daughter went to work in the Saudi Arabian Education Mission, she had opportunities to talk with leaders in the mosque. She called me on the phone to tell me about her conversion. My first reaction was not surprise but concern about how she would deal with the discrimination. She has elected to wear the traditional apparel including covering her head, but she seems to deal with the level of bias she has encountered to date. Seeing how my daughter has adjusted helps me not worry.

Our daughter first became a Muslim, then later got married. The fact that he was younger than she and not established in a career were points of greater concern than the religious issue. This was a third marriage for her. The first ended in divorce. The second to an Egyptian Muslim was dissolved within the Muslim tradition. This one was a quiet marriage, also within the Muslim tradition.

At first there was some distancing among family [members] and her marriage and husband took awhile to accept, but this worked both ways for him too. Today everyone is very open. The sisters have become exceptionally close although at times some strain exists with the brothers–in–law.

Values and belief systems pose very little difficulty, but do require lots of tolerance and acceptance on the part of everyone. Our daughter is not evangelical about her

Muslim beliefs—she seeks acceptance, not conversion. This helps. Communication is great. We are all well–read and love to share ideas about life, politics, and world affairs.

This experience has had very little effect on my theology and religious commitment. I am well–versed in theology and religion. I have always lived a life of understanding and tolerance. I enjoy knowing about the belief systems of others and have always actively sought to be informed. My present religious orientation is that of an agnostic—identity is with a unitarian fellowship.

At holidays each person does his or her own thing. The family gatherings are not focused upon religion. We celebrate life and living. We share food. The dietary habits and traditions of Muslim and Jewish are very similar. We are not included in their holidays but acknowledge occasions and respect traditions. We live in a household where shoes are removed, diet is mostly vegetarian with some lamb, chicken, and fish. So these matters are natural. Religious objects and art are not part of our household and our daughter's family does not impose these upon us.

The two grandchildren are great. We do truly enjoy them and they are a real source of pleasure.

My greatest concern is discrimination toward her and the grandchildren. My wife lived with this as a child —Jewish in a non–Jewish world. It can be cruel; many so–called Christians hate a lot and hurt others with it. Our son–in–law is Palestinian and most members of his family, including parents, now live in the USA. I have real concerns about prospects for a very assertive daughter if a decision were made to live in the Middle East.

My hope for my relationship with my daughter is that it will continue as it is today and that we will be able to have a positive, accepting relationship with grandchildren.

Ours is unique with a mixture of Muslim, Jewish, and Unitarian. We are necessarily tolerant.

The strength of this story is the family's openness to diversity and the added dimension brought to the family by the daughter. This household already embraced religious differences and was able to open the boundaries to accept yet another style of life. Even then, there was need for adjustment and work on the part of both the daughter and her family with the family of origin.

Story 3: From Devastation to Acceptance

In the next family the mother goes from devastation to a very warm acceptance of what her daughter has chosen, but it has happened over a period of many years. The daughter has been Muslim for 12 years. Upon first learning about their daughter becoming Muslim, the mother rated her own feelings regarding the conversion as a 1; the father, a 4. However, both of them rated their feelings at 8 at the time of the questionnaire. The mother shares her story.

When our daughter went to an out–of–city [church] college, we felt confident we were sending her to an environment as close to our home life as possible. We met her new friend from [a Middle Eastern country] when we visited her and liked him. We even invited him to our home one weekend. We never thought that this would become a serious relationship. We thought this daughter was the strongest of all four children when it came to religion. Four months later she told us that she was no longer attending Mass. The next semester when this friend transferred to another college, she wanted to do the same, but we refused to let her. We were hoping this would be the end of the relationship and that she would come out of the "phase" she was in.

The next summer, the friend rented an apartment in our home town, and our daughter moved in with her grandmother since we were not getting along very well. She announced to us the latter part of June that she was going to marry him in August, "with or without us." We reluctantly went along with the plans but none of us believed this wedding would ever happen. But it did happen at our home by a judge which was a compromise since she had not yet converted to Islam. His parents had not yet been told of the marriage, so we did not have the support from his family to confirm our objections.

It was a few months later she told us she was converting. I responded to that news with anger, hurt, and fear. The anger was aimed at my son–in–law mostly since we were convinced that our daughter never would have made this decision unless she had been brainwashed. It hurt because it appeared at the time to be so easy for her to give up a lifetime of instruction and living with our lives centered around Jesus Christ. The fact that she could just reject these teachings in just a few months was devastating. The fear at first was that our other children might do the same since she was the oldest child, and they all looked up to her and respected her opinions.

As time went on we became more aware of the Middle East and listened carefully to the news and reports of terrorists from that area. Then the fear was for her. As long as her husband was in college, we felt certain they would not leave the United States, but we did not know what might happen when he was finished. After they had their first son, we were more afraid than ever that he [her husband] would want to take them to his country. This fear somewhat was eased when he became an American citizen. We tried to relax a little and try trusting. We were not only worried about her earthly life but her heavenly life as well.

The scripture that kept haunting me was John 14:6: "I am the way, and the truth, and the life; no one comes to the father but through me." I decided that if the scripture was bothering me, it was going to have to be another scripture that relieved me. So I began reading that chapter word by word. In the very first verse I got the inspiration I needed. "Do not let your hearts be troubled. Have faith in God and faith in me. In my Father's house there are many dwelling places." This scripture said to me that if there are many dwelling places then there must be many roads leading to these places. Jesus is preparing a place for Christians and Mohammad is preparing a place for Muslims. God just picked a different road for our daughter to follow, and she is following it the best she can. Which is exactly what we are all trying to do. No one in this family will try to add obstacles or bumps in her road to make it more difficult for her. This was the main story that helped me adjust.

I'm going to add a little story that helped confirm my insights. One day my oldest grandson was very insistent that I learn the Arabic language. When I asked him why he thought I should, he responded, "Because when you die the angels will come and ask you certain questions in Arabic, and you will have to know how to answer them or you will go to hell." I knew by the tone of his voice that my answer to him had to be a good one, and it turned out to be the answer to myself also. I told him, "We each have our own private angels that know exactly what is in our hearts. I will know the answers to my angel's questions, and you will know the answers to yours." He appeared relieved and I felt very relieved.

To me the answer to the differences in our faith is just that simple. It was also helpful seeing our daughter as a mother and knowing that many of our basic values were being passed on. She is a very caring and delightful daughter and a wonderful mother of now two boys ages 10 and 3. We still have a loving relationship that all of us work very hard to keep. We have a good family foundation, and I'm sure it will withstand any differences we may face in years to come.

We are fortunate that they do partake in family Christmas festivities. They think of it as their "Eid" sharing time with us. When Eid really arrives, they share it with her husband's family and friends. I don't know if that will last forever, but for now that is how we handle it. We do not celebrate Islamic celebrations with them only to acknowledge them and respect the value they have in their lives.

Each family's story is different, but in these three stories each family wants to work with the situation. Although cares and concerns are still present, they are working out how to relate.   As family, we are always in relationship whether it is positive or negative. Parents may have feelings of betrayal, of being wounded or fractured. The way parents react to the daughter may cause the same feelings in her. At some point in the process of reconciliation there has to be a decision of how to handle the hurt and how to allow that to affect oneself. Many times we are mindless about our relationship and are not aware of how we are treating others. We are so quick to defend ourselves, so quick to pull our heads into our shells like a turtle, so resistant at times to anything that is outside our understanding.

Steps Toward Reconciliation

There are common threads in the three stories shared by these parents that are played out differently in each situation. These common threads can help us navigate in positive ways through relationship building and maintainance in our own situations of reconciliation.

First, there was an innate yearning to maintain the relationship even though deep hurt and separation had occurred. In Story 1 the mother states that "we loved her and wanted to continue being a part of her life." My own experience of reconciliation was one of wanting to make the relationship good. It didn't happen immediately. In fact it would have been easy to have gotten stuck in the resistance mode, which was my first reaction. I was so angry and hurt that I wanted to walk away from Jodi and Reza, get them out of my life, and never have to deal with them and "that problem" again. For me that phase of wanting to completely reject them lasted only a short time—just overnight. How grateful I am for the experience that helped direct me towards a desire for healing to take place. It still hurt and it took months of grieving to feel okay; it took several years to come to a comfortable level of acceptance.

Another thread that assisted in rebuilding the relationship was the willingness to try to understand what the daughter was choosing. In her deep longing for release, one mother searched the scriptures and found help that kept the lines for acceptance open. This may be an almost forced effort, an act of the will at first, to take this step of openness, but parents with a strong sense of values should be able to risk hearing and seeing and feeling what their daughter is experiencing. The daughter may have "moved" too far away from the family to the point that there are feelings she has transgressed against the family, and the family actually feels injured. Each family member must make the decision of how to react. Some things the daughter has chosen may be beyond the capacity of the family to accept. In that case, retreat may be the best approach.

In this step of trying to understand, one can search out resources to read and learn about what the daughter has chosen. A caution here: what is read may reflect Western views or may be culturally slanted. There are also various interpretations within the Muslim community, and they don't always agree. Books might be selected from the bibliography at the end of this book or from suggestions offered by the Muslim daughter. This is prime time to start thinking through a personal theology and belief system and strengthen one's own spiritual life. Many times we have accepted beliefs we haven't even examined; we have heard our preacher say it or it was on a religious program or "that's the way Grandma believed."

With the desire to reconcile in place and the openness to understand, one then needs to identify and confront the factors that are important from the parents' point of view and to identify their feelings whether it be rejection, frustration or lack of control. The family members may need to be gentle with themselves until strong enough to start the journey of relationship–building again, taking time to work through the denial, the anger, and the depression. Some members of the family may even need to seek out counseling to help work through feelings of anger or grief.

One factor that may be identified is anger which is a natural emotion in such circumstances, but it is important to express it in appropriate ways, so that healing and reconciliation can happen. Even in this situation, God's healing love and forgiveness is present, and family members can find release and can come to a sense of the problem by letting go of the hurt; otherwise there will be feelings of being burdened and diseased.

Another factor that may be identified as a concern is our inability to let go of control, to let go of the young adult offspring which is a difficult task for many parents whether or not their daughter has turned to Islam. A parent may already be experiencing anxiety, loss, and grief as a natural phenomenon of letting go. When a daughter makes choices with which the parents are so unfamiliar, it may compound the situation with feelings of fear, uncertainty, and failure. It is important to understand that some of the feelings that a parent is experiencing may not be directly related to the daughter's conversion.

Still another factor is that the daughter may not be in a readiness mode to work on the relationship, and thus, there is the possibility for more feelings of rejection on our part. She may be trying to gain strength and re-freeze in the new roles she has chosen before facing the power of her parents. Many elements of change may be affecting her at once—education or work, new religion, new cultural expectations, new marriage, the transition into adulthood. For most of the women in the study, several of these factors were present.

The fourth element is that of hope. These situations are not usually settled immediately. There will be a lot of steps forward and then some steps backwards in building and maintaining the relationship. There may be times when the daughter has to retreat and is not ready to continue work on the relationship. Likewise, there will be instances when we must take time for personal grief and growth while keeping the lines of communication open. It is the sense of hope that allows us to be patient with our daughter as we must be with ourselves.

Well–meaning friends and relatives may dash our hope as they react with comments like the following:

"Oh, your poor daughter—she will go to hell. We will pray for her."

"All women are treated so terribly over there."

"What will she do if the husband leaves her and takes the children to his country?"

"That is just about the worst thing that could happen."

Such reactions are not meant to hurt but to sympathize and reinforce what they perceive as our reality. On the other hand, some people are able to be listeners, to question, to empathize with our concerns. Talking with them helps us reflect what we are feeling and helps clarify the confusion within us.

If we can be cognizant of these common threads or basic steps of opening ourselves by desiring to relate, by being open to understanding and acceptance, by identifying and confronting our own feelings, and by remaining hopeful, then we are in a growth mode for reconciliation. We can thus deal with our anger, fears, and grief; we can find help through the passage of time. Using techniques of prayer, relaxation, calmness, and visualization can help us keep from sinking into depths of despair and wallowing in it. Even though we may not want to join our daughter in her path, we will be able to journey with her from our own pathway.

7. Following the Path into Marriage
When Two Become One in Islam

From the first moment Jodi and Reza told us they wanted to get married, they made it clear that they intended to live in his homeland, Iran. It was at the time that American hostages were being held captive in Iran, and relations between Iran and America were not good. That was really frightening to me. The fact that he was Muslim seemed less important because we anticipated that he would probably convert to Christianity. Besides, we really respected and liked this young man.

The dreaded day had finally arrived. Reza was taking Jodi to Iran to live just as they said they would when they got engaged. They had made a trip to Iran early in their marriage, but now that Reza had his bachelor's degree in engineering plus a master's degree in industrial technology and Jodi had completed her bachelor's degree in nursing, they were ready to go. The war between Iraq and Iran was still being waged. It just didn't seem safe. So far away—would I ever see her again? The scene from *Fiddler on the Roof* again flooded my mind as I pictured Tevya with his second daughter at the train stop waiting to send her off on the train to Siberia to be with her husband. I heard again the words of his daughter's song, "Far From the Home I Love."

Jodi and Reza sold everything they had except for what they could carry in the four huge suitcases that they would take with them to start life in Iran. They spent the last night with us. They were so excited and happy! Seeing them off that next morning at the airport was one of the hardest things I had ever done. I felt like Jodi was going out of our lives for good. I wanted to lie down on the airport floor and kick and scream. But I kept control until we got to the car where I could safely fall apart. She was gone. I would never see her again. It was as if she were dead. This marriage had torn her from me, taking her to a strange, war-torn land.

But life went on, and I went off on a work trip to Canada. Joe called me there to tell me Jodi had called. A dam had broken in a mountain above Teheran, and the water had come through the area where they were living with Reza's parents. Over a thousand people had been killed by the surging water and mud slide, and among the dead was Reza's father who had been drowned in the basement apartment where the family lived. Most things in the apartment were ruined as it was under several feet of mud and water. The family rescued their father's body from the water, cleaned the apartment, and tried to save what they could.

I felt a deep sadness. Yes, I was sad about Reza's father, but I was also overwhelmed with another kind of grief. If Jodi had lost everything she had taken with her to Iran, how could she ever remember who we were or her former life? She had nothing left to remind her—all her pictures were gone, all her keepsakes, her papers. I was sure that she would forget, over time, who we were and who she had been. Now her family would be Reza's family, and no doubt we would eventually lose contact.

Three months later we received another call. Jodi and Reza were coming back to the United States. The economy in Iran was difficult as a result of the war. They began to realize that they needed more time to build their financial strength before making the commitment to live in Iran. What a celebration for us! They were coming back. We would have our Jodi and Reza back.

We have had many years now together in the same metropolitan area. The respect and love we had for Reza from the beginning has grown and matured. The role Reza seems to express in his family with his wife and children is similar to that of conservative Christians who feel the responsibility to be head of the family. He takes seriously that leadership for the family while at the same time encouraging Jodi to be a participating partner in their decisions.

If we were to describe all Muslim husbands by the model presented to us by our son–in–law, we would tell you they are gentle, strong, kind, intelligent, courteous, happy, dependable, nurturing. We are amazed at his knowledge and commitment to practice his religion, his desire that his children grow up to be practicing Muslims and be protected from bad images on TV or movies, his feeling of responsibility to be sure his family is cared for, and his dependable handling of finances. There is also his strong feeling for his family of origin and connectedness to his country of origin.

❖ ❖ ❖

Just as the value of a strong male role model in the home and family is important in the Christian family, so is this strength fostered in the Muslim family. The husband is encouraged to be a strong force in the family, to provide the financial support for the family, and to give leadership in decision–making and religious practices.

Some of the women questioned converted to Islam while they were still single, and they said it was important to them that they marry a Muslim. On the other hand, a non–Muslim woman's introduction to Islam may have come at the time she married a Muslim man. In other instances, a prior interest in Islam may have opened the way for a non–Muslim woman to develop a relationship with a Muslim man.

The husbands in my survey came originally from a variety of countries: Iran, Iraq, Syria, Egypt, Jordan, Palestine, Kuwait, India, Turkey, Lebanon, Pakistan, Kenya, Afghanistan, Oman, Tunisia, Morocco, and United States of America. Many of the men now hold United States or Canadian citizenship and all are well–educated. Some plan to take their families back to their country of origin or are already living there; others are committed to living in the United States or Canada with hopes of being in a city where there are large Muslim communities in which to worship and to raise their children.

One of the women who was single when she responded to the questionnaire wrote later to tell me that she had married a wonderful Egyptian man who extended to her and her family care and respect.

❖You are probably wondering why I am telling you all of this. I just want you to understand that in Islam the institution of marriage is what has helped me to practice my religion to the fullest amount possible. As an American convert, I found it very hard at first to be a good Muslim and follow all the changes I had to make in my life, even though I did do it gradually. Now with my husband, I feel even more fulfilled. In my heart I know that I have made the right decision. I am most lucky to not have to decide between my family and Islam (because Islam would have won), but I am most lucky because Allah has guided me to the right path. I am not saying I have no problems, but all I do now is look into my heart and read Qur'an and I feel that all is better.

Finding a Muslim Husband

The couples met in a variety of settings just as is common in America—at college, in the job setting, at social activities, or through friends. Here are some stories of those meetings.

❖I met my husband playing Bingo. I was sitting by a family friend and it so happened he knew her too. He had a nice smile and was easy to talk to. I had come from a disastrous relationship with an abusive man nine years my senior but many years my junior in maturity. When I met this next man I was in such a bad frame of mind about men it is a wonder I considered marriage again. He didn't mention sex or make remarks or grab my body parts or call me his ol' lady in public. It was refreshing to be treated in such a way. He would never take me anywhere without a chaperon as a witness that he was a gentleman. I felt respect and I liked it.

❖I met my husband at college. He was very polite (I noticed that right way) and very good looking. I really wasn't looking for anyone when we met but the first thing I noticed in him, which was always on the top of my list, was his importance of family (loyalty, respect) toward mother and father. He answered questions so patiently.

❖I met my husband at the community college I was attending. He was the grill cook. Something just clicked between us. He was kind and nice to talk to. He had a religious feeling about him and was mature in his ideas. Of course, I thought he was handsome too. I liked the lifestyle he offered of a family–based society. I especially thought he was my friend and we agreed easily on many matters including religious. He was a catalyst for my own personal exploration.

❖I tutored him in English. He helped me study Islam, but when I converted I could no longer see him—he fully respected my decision to stop seeing him once I became Muslim. Later, several people noticed a "perfect match" for me in the mosque and it turned out to be the same man I had tutored and who had brought me to Islam. I found him to be sincere, gentle, generous, and patient. If ever there would be a "soul mate" for me, he's the one. He has filled the "holes" of loneliness and need for unconditional love that had not been filled before. My family accepted him completely from the day they met him. They love him dearly, and he is a friend to all of them.

❖My husband and I met when we worked in the same restaurant. I was a waitress and he was a dishwasher. He was new in the country and didn't speak English. He seemed honest, uncomplicated, hard–working, and generous.

❖I met my husband while in college. We worked at the same Mexican food restaurant. I was attracted to him because he was very hard–working, smart, and conducted himself politely. I was in need of a person to think I was wonderful. He put me on a pedestal and treated me like a queen (even though we were dirt poor) with respect and dignity.

Some of the women had already converted to Islam while still single and met their husbands in other ways. One common way of finding a husband or wife is through advertising in an Islamic magazine or at a matrimonial booth at a Muslim conference. It is not unusual for one who is ready to get married to let Muslim friends know so they can help in looking for a suitable mate. The following excerpts from the questionnaires provide a good overview of the Muslim/Muslim relationship and marriage.

❖I met my husband through the imam of the mosque. I accepted him because he was religious. Nothing else really mattered. He had no part in my conversion for I was already a Muslim. My marriage ceremony was all Islamic. I talked to him for two weeks and then decided to marry him two days before Ramadan 1991.

❖My marriage was arranged by my request in order to have support (religiously) to help me learn about my deen (my obligations). I asked my wali (the one who arranged the marriage) that the man be a good practicing Muslim which was the only characteristic he needed. I wanted a husband that would teach me about Islam in depth and to remind me always of Allah (SWT). I was already Muslim.

My family didn't know him before the marriage. They met him two days before the ceremony, and he asked my parents' permission to marry me the day before. They didn't like him. Now they tolerate him only.

My husband–to–be first came to see me on a Friday night and we were married on the following Sunday afternoon. At our ceremony we invited friends and family. Our wedding was an Islamic wedding. I wore an Islamic dress, not a white gown. We were in separate rooms. The imam came and asked me if I accept [the man] and what I wanted for my mahar [dowry]. I heard him give a speech about the importance of marriage. At that point my mom walked out saying what a big farce the wedding was. Of course, I cried and was hurt, but we continued the wedding but at a faster pace.

❖I met my husband through a marriage ad in an Islamic magazine. A friend of his had put the ad in. [I was too late in responding to the ad for that man, but the] friend gave my letter to [another man,] the one who is now my husband because he was also wanting to get married. We talked on the phone ten to twelve hours a week for six weeks; then he flew to Kansas. We were about 90 percent sure about marriage even before we met, but had to meet to know for sure. We got engaged that day, and did the Islamic marriage (nikkah) two days later.

I was looking for someone who was a strong Muslim, both in theory and practice—one who lived his life Islamically, regardless of how others around him lived. I wanted someone who would be a good provider, because in a marriage it is the man who provides the family with everything, even if the woman has money. I had heard many stories about men who didn't work, or wanted the wife to support them, so I wanted to make sure my husband would work hard for us. The more I got to know about him, the more he seemed to fit this. I had been straight–forward in my letter about wanting a strong Muslim, that I was divorced with a child, (in case it was someone wanting a young virgin), and enclosed my photo. Even though I didn't ask for his photo right away, he sent one to me. Looks are not important. He and I got to know each other very well on the phone, talking about many things about our lives—Islam, current events (including some that involved Muslims), etc. I made sure his family would accept an American wife [he was from a Muslim country], even one who has divorced with one child from that marriage. But he assured me that wouldn't make a bit of difference to them, that they all chose their mates, and some chose mates from other countries.

We became very close through our phone conversation, and I always looked forward to him calling. If I had a bad day, I wanted to tell him about it so I would feel better. It was like an old–fashioned courtship. Our passions didn't get in the way of getting to know each other. When we met, we realized we were right for each other, and the friendship and affection we felt for each other turned to love. Islam does not allow dating, pre–marital sex, etc. This is a great way to get to know someone, and see if you get along with each other. That is the most important [step], getting to know if someone else is on your level, Islamically and personally. If they are, you will love them and be attracted to them.

I wanted someone who was gentle and loving, and I found someone like that. He does not yell at me or hit me, as is the stereotype of Arab men. I have to admit, I thought that all Arab men were controlling and violent, but they are not. He tells me he loves me, and makes sure I know that he does. He is very caring and concerned.

Entering Into a Muslim Marriage

If the couple survives family objections during the courtship period, they prepare to enter into marriage. It is often difficult for the parents of the woman marrying a Muslim from another country. They may feel suspicious of the man's intentions and express fear for their daughter. First–time meetings between the male suitor and the woman's family may be strained. However, in many cases among this sample of women, the family, too, grew to accept and establish a friendship with the husband.

✤My parents were unsure about my husband as they didn't get to meet him in person until the night we married. We purposely spent a few days (after our marriage) with them so they could get to know him better. They have grown to love him dearly. In fact, in my father's eyes, he is the son he never had. My mother has confessed that she couldn't wish a nicer husband for me. Considering their veritable objections when they first discovered how I found him, my family has espoused my husband as one of their own.

In the survey I asked for positive stories of those converting to Islam. This is not to ignore the reports of the poor relationships that exist. One woman called me on the phone after receiving the questionnaire and said she couldn't give her name or answer the questionnaire because her experience had not been positive. In fact, she had been married to two different Muslims, both well–educated and one a physician. Both beat her and abused her badly. She was in hiding, afraid for her life.

It is not my intent to glorify Muslim marriage, but I certainly recognize that all Muslim marriages are not catastrophes as the media would lead us to believe. My intention in writing this is to share some positive experiences which contrast with the negative stories in order to present a more balanced picture. Among Muslims there are good, bad, and in–between marriages just like that of other religions and cultures, and abusive relationships may be found. There are even those men from other countries who marry only to have access to the green card (allowing the non–citizen to stay in the United States and work).

❖I joined a pen pal club from a newspaper ad and got a letter from an Arab college student. He proposed and I fell for it. He basically married me to get my virginity and his green card. After our divorce I was living in Tennessee. Friends introduced me to another Muslim. He was a religious, simple guy—answered all my questions right, and I wanted a husband and children of my own. My parents were skeptical before our marriage because they didn't think he was any different from my first husband who was Muslim. They accept him now and our three–year–old son. We had a simple marriage ceremony at the Islamic Center. Then we went out to eat at Ponderosa Steak House. The reception was fancier but only attended by a few friends of ours. I had a sisters' bachelorette party the night before—fun! It was traditionally Islamic. Then we went to New York for two weeks for our honeymoon.

❖I was married before to a Muslim and had a very bad marriage. For five years I was physically and emotionally abused. My advice for anyone who wants to marry is to have a wali to check the brothers [brothers are the Muslim men] that want to marry. This marriage was bad. After we married he prayed once, got his green card, flirted with women, and finally became a citizen. He has a restaurant, married a Muslima from Singapore and brought his family here—all thanks to me being born in the U.S.A. I am now *happily* married to another Muslim.

A Muslim marriage for the women surveyed was by and large very positive, beginning with the ceremony itself, which often differed significantly from traditional western styles. Sometimes the wedding ceremony itself added to the fears and hurts of the family. Families dream of walking their daughter up the aisle of the church and having the minister join her to a man of whom they approve. It will be a sacrament in the Christian tradition with the reception and gifts and fellowship following.

The stories of weddings between a non–Muslim and a Muslim, however, illustrate many differences and varieties of situations. Some did have the large weddings (often blamed on satisfying the parents), but there were also elopements, small weddings before the justice of the peace, and/or Muslim ceremonies.

❖We had a special ceremony for a Muslim marrying a non–Muslim (informal) which is called a term marriage. Our term was for ninety–nine years. It was just us and two friends. Then we had a wedding for my family in my parents' church. My father married us and did not refer to Jesus. He was respective of my husband's needs. It was very nice and family–oriented. There were not many problems because I was not Muslim and my husband was not strongly practicing. We also had a third wedding after I became Muslim to celebrate our permanent standing as two Muslims married to each other.

❖My family never expressed any opposition to my marriage or to my husband. We were not close. My mother only asked me if I was happy. When I answered yes, she said so was she.

Our marriage was performed by a Baptist minister. Because I had not belonged to any church for many years, I didn't know a minister, so we asked the minister from the church that my roommates attended at the time. It was very simple. We asked to read the ceremony beforehand. The only change we asked for was that the minister replace the words, "In Jesus' name" to "In God's name." The nicest part was the Arab tradition afterwards with singing and dancing.

❖We were married by a justice of the peace at a court-house without my family and with only friends as witnesses. Then a few months later we were married by a shaikh [Muslim religious leader] in a short ceremony with only one witness.

❖There were no cultural elements in our wedding such as cutting and eating cake or sprinkling sugar over our heads. Our wedding was the most basic Islamic marriage, where two people find the need to become partners in life and agree before God to live and work together in harmony and stay away from sins. He read the words of the marriage ceremony in Arabic and I agreed to the marriage. For my dowry he promised to give me my own Arabic Qur'an, which he gave to me sometime later. He gave me items for prayer, including a prayer carpet. After we were married, according to the law of Islam, we went to the county courthouse and were married by a judge. (In Islam, Muslims are advised to follow the rules of the country in which they reside as long as these laws are not contrary to Islam.)

❖We had a ceremony at my church not geared to any particular faith. We also had a nikkah performed at the mosque the day before our wedding ceremony.

❖Our marriage ceremony was beautiful! Perfect as others describe it. The day was perfect, sunshine and cool. A string quartet, mansion for a venue, and excellent catered brunch buffet. I understand that it is typical to have Arabic music played at a reception and both of us were in agreement that most of our guests would have been put off by it so we decided on strings. Other than two items, our ceremony was an entirely Islamic ceremony. The two elements that made it not completely Islamic were my father giving me away and that we had guests attend the ceremony. I am glad we had Christian guests at the ceremony because then part of the mystery surrounding Islam was removed.

Relating to the Husband's Family

Another factor is the power that the family of the husband has over acceptance of the wife. Of course, this is something we all have to do in marriage—to work out the relationship with our in–laws, but in this situation there is the added dimension of cultural differences. There is a strong attachment by most of the men to their families of origin and to their homelands, and what that family feels in accepting the wife may be very important. Sometimes it is strong enough to break up a marriage if families disapprove; some learn to live with a poor relationship with the husband's family, but the majority of these women respondents found love, acceptance, and pleasure in knowing their husband's family. They reported good communication between the families by letter and telephone and visits back to the husband's homeland. At times the relatives come to visit or reside in the United States or Canada.

❖I have met my husband's family. I was scared to death to meet them—they had bad ideas about American women. They were shocked to see that I cover my face—they were visibly uncomfortable about it. Not a warm welcome, but no one tried to kill me!

We live in my husband's family's home (in his country of origin). I have been here a year, and I have not been accepted—only a few of them have wholeheartedly welcomed me. Most of them have a fear that one day I'll leave and take the kids.

My husband and I truly felt I would be another one of the gang. Well, I'm not even close! I'm not sure I'll ever fit in as a true family member. As we anticipated, we have a lot of problems regarding Islamic practices. My husband's family is very westernized. The benefits of being near them have been for my husband and the kids—a bigger framework to fit into as full, permanent family members.

❖My husband's family was there when we married. His mother is Brazilian and converted upon her marriage so they are sympathetic to some of the difficulties. They are living in the U.S. now and will probably (when we can afford a big enough place) live part of the year with us. They will help the children and me with Arabic and also Portuguese. The difficulties will be their poor diet and exercise habits. I'm a health food nut (except for chocolate!) and my husband gets tense and weird around his father but this is improving.

We help support them financially and that does make our lives harder, but they lost everything in '67 war and again in the Gulf War. They were in Kuwait. They are simple people and so are we.

❖My husband's mother is very dear to me and we all cry very hard when the time comes for us to leave. It is like when I visit and leave my own family. Both my parents and his family care deeply for each other and mine sends gifts and calls when we are there.

❖I met my husband's family on a trip we made to his country. They are wonderful people, and they have been completely accepting even though I was a divorced American woman with kids who was not even Muslim, because I was important to their son and brother.

There are some areas that I have more or less difficulty fitting in. I'll never get used to having 35 and more relatives who don't think they have to knock, and think our private business is theirs. And I've never gotten comfortable taking off with the women for days at a time at larger gatherings. I made them assign a room to my family at a family wedding so I could get my own husband and children together if I wanted to—weird idea, I know. My husband puts up with my idiosyncrasies fairly well most of the time, and when he doesn't, his mother tells him he had better work out a middle ground with me!

The benefits of relating to his family are that they are really a family with all the good and bad features thereof —something I had not really ever had before in my own family.

❖I met dozens of relatives in the first few weeks of being in Egypt, and it was a very stressful experience. Now I can say that his family and I get along well, and I am quite attached to them after having lived with them by myself for two months while my husband was in Saudi working. They've also accepted me, and feel comfortable with me, I think mostly because I showed them I was respectful of them and that I loved their son. The benefit is that I'll learn Arabic. The problem is always being aware of the fact that they're wary of Americans in general.

There are those who are even more warmly accepted by their husband's family than by their own. The following letter was written by one woman to her friend in the United States during a visit by the woman and her husband to his parents in Iran.

❖I've been here about one week now and everything is so wonderful. I have adopted my mother–in–law for my own. She is so wonderful. This first week has been interesting, meeting his family and trying to remember what customs to use and when. So far my husband has said that every-one says they love me, and I feel like I have been ac-cepted. They treat me like a queen. My mother–in–law kisses me all the time and waits on me hand and foot. Not knowing for sure what to expect when I got here, I did a lot of unnecessary worrying.

We were met at the airport by a lot of his family and it was a very touching moment, one I'll never forget. Mama is like an angel. I can't believe we waited so long to see her. I have spent a lot of time with tears because of what I see here. The family system here is unique with closeness that is beyond words. Some of my tears are due to the fact that I felt more love in one week from his family than from my own flesh who didn't even bother to say goodbye.

Blending Cultures

The women are learning to be Muslim and at the same time, if married to a man from another country, may be incorporating many new cultural elements into the family. The women indicate a blend of American culture, the husband's background traditions, and an effort to interpret all these Islamically.

❖Many traditions including those about pets; the way we cook, bathe, and talk; and all manners are from my husband's traditions. My childhood lifestyles are almost 100 percent different now and are not an accepted part of our traditions.

❖In some ways our life has taken on much Iranian traditions and culture, including the food we eat and the way the food is prepared, and my hijab [there are many ways to wear hijab]. Many things I do are Iranian but my mannerisms and thinking are still very American.

❖There is a blend—no shoes in the house, the manner of washing after using the toilet, answering the phone assalamu alaikum (the common greeting among Muslims)—these are mostly Islamic customs. We eat Persian foods about 75 percent of the time.

❖Our daily life really doesn't include Iraqi culture —maybe a little Arab culture though. Our children play games in Arabic that my husband played when he was small. At least twice a week my husband teaches the children Arabic and Qur'an.

❖Our daily life includes very much the traditions and culture of my husband's country, Syria. Most of my friends are from other countries. Their cultures are also an influence. Most important, my husband's mother is with us for extended visits. She always brings a part of Syria with her. When she is not here, our ways are pretty much American–Muslim. This is a combination of cultures.

❖My husband encourages us to learn Arabic and likewise he tries to learn Americanisms such as children's play songs, poems, sayings. We try to blend our cultures comfortably, and we are both accustomed to being around people from other cultures and languages than our own.

❖The only culture is Islam. I even try not to follow the American culture. I try to put Islam first in everything I do. My husband's family is very stuck in tradition and Indian culture. This gave us many problems on our visit.

❖Our everyday life includes traditions or culture from Iran. How can it not; my husband is Iranian. That will never change. He tells stories, we sing songs, and we eat a lot of Iranian foods.

❖Our daily life is just normal everyday living. What is different about our family is that we do try to look at life from an Islamic point of view, and we explain Islam to our children using events that happen in our daily lives.

❖Since we are both Muslim, Islam is the main impact on our family. Of course, it is meshed with the foods from his country and small sayings when we wake up, bathe, and sleep. I feel I have created my traditions in our family because I really want an Islamically–oriented family. We have made many new traditions. My husband is very lonely here in America. He misses his family so badly which he left when he was eighteen years old. So I try to make up for his sadness by taking my house role very seriously and lovingly.

The women in this survey seemed relatively happy with their marriages at the time they responded to the questionnaire. They were attracted to these Muslim men from other countries by a variety of characteristics which they saw as mature and positive. Not all the women were married to Muslim men at the time of their conversion; some converted while still single and later wanted to be married to a practicing Muslim. As in any religion, the couple being of "like minds" in their religious practice helps to bring harmony and stability to their lives together.

8. Raising Children in Another Path
Muslim Children in American Society

We had taken our children with us to the church campgrounds for annual family church camps during the years our children were growing up. Jodi also went to these campgrounds for youth camps. These were the grounds where many good growing experiences in her spiritual life had occurred during childhood and youth. At the campfires, at the prayer services, in the classes, in the study of the scriptures, and in the good fellowship of other Christian friends her life had been impressed by challenges to worship and to follow God.

It was when she was fifteen and attending a youth camp that she wrote a poem that she felt came to her as inspiration. This poem speaks to her life in a very special way.

THE INSPIRATION

Wherever I'm at, it is my home;
The people I'm with, my family.
There'll be different things
    Wherever I roam,
    Wherever I go, I'll go happily.
Don't worry about me—I don't walk alone
For God is walking beside me,
And as we walk along

We speak in soft tones;
Together we keep each other company.

I'll go where he wants, wherever I'm led—
Though the roads may be long and dreary.
I'll not remember the harsh words that are said,
But the people I've sought to help
Who are weary.
The times I'll remember will be happy ones,
No matter what others will say.
The bad that there is
Will not overcome
For God's with me all the way.
Jodi C. Anway
June, 1978

We were going to the same campgrounds again for the weekend, but it was different this time—a different group of people. Jodi and Reza had scheduled the campgrounds for their Islamic group. We were invited to go, and it would be fun to help with some of the cooking, visit with the people, and be there to help out with our grandchild. We were the only non-Muslims present and no one seemed to care that I wasn't wearing a scarf to cover my hair.

The weekend with the Muslim people was very comfortable. These were mostly young adults with their children. The women all covered their heads with the hijab, the men were modestly dressed, and the children loved being in the out-of-doors. The swimming pool was a great attraction, but the rules were special this weekend. Blankets were hung on the fence to give privacy as the women went swimming together with the younger children. The men and older boys went in at a different time.

At meal times we all ate together in the mess hall enjoying the interaction of visiting and sharing. There was an air of friendliness and cooperation as both men and women worked in the kitchen, took care of children, fished in the lake, took walks, and generally enjoyed each other. Both men and women showed care and respect in their relationships toward each other as they observed the Muslim code of conduct. I really wasn't even aware of how that was carried out except that the men seemed to congregate together as did the women.

I saw them at prayer in the dining hall several times as they lined up, men grouped together with the older boys, the women together, and the young children merrily going their way among the people but disturbing no one in their prayers. This was the same dining hall where I had come to women's retreats and studied and prayed and had fellowship. I felt a kinship with these people. They were people of God who had come to these grounds that were sacred to me, and they too were offering up their prayers, their commitment, their desire to live a good life, just as I had done so many times in the years past.

It pleased me to know that our grandchildren were being raised in a family with that kind of commitment to God and to family. One day at my daughter's, I was sitting on the bed by grandbaby Fatemeh. Jodi was in the same room doing her noon–day prayers recited in the Arabic language. She had her prayer garments on and was performing her prayers on the special prayer rug. My grandson, Emaun, almost four years old at the time, crawled up by me. He had listened to Baba (what he calls his father) and Mama recite the prayers to God in Arabic several times a day in his few years of life. Emaun said to me, "Grandma, do you do namaz?"

"Are those the prayers, Emaun?"

"Yes," he answered.

"Well, I pray to God, but I do it in a different way."

"What do you say, Grandma?"

I answered that I make up my own prayers to God. Now Emaun knew that I only speak English and not the language of his Baba, which is Farsi, or the language of their prayers, Arabic. So to my reply that I made up my prayers to God, Emaun said, "But

Grandma, God doesn't know English." Later Jodi talked with him
to help him understand that God knows all languages.

❖ ❖ ❖

Islam is introduced to the newborn in the earliest moments of
the child's life as the father or other able adult whispers into the
child's ears "God is the Most Great. . . . I witness there is no God
but Allah. . . . and Mohammad is the Messenger of Allah. . . .
Hasten to prayer. . . . Hasten to success. . . . God is the Most
Great." A sheep is often sacrificed during the early days or months
after a child's birth, and the meat is distributed to the needy. The
choice of a good name is important so that it might influence the
child in a positive way. It is recommended that boys be
circumcised. The parents are responsible for teaching their
children to pray and to preform the proper ablutions by age nine.
It is a Muslim belief that the parents will be rewarded by God with
many blessings and forgiveness of sins if good effort is made in
child–rearing.

The responses of the women who have children indicate that
one of their most important roles and obligations is to be a
responsible parent. From modeling behaviors to their commitment
and daily training, they want to raise their children to continue the
tradition of being Muslim and to practice those beliefs in a
committed way. I see that daily training and modeling evident with
our grandson.

The women indicated that the responsibility they have in their
roles as wife and mother is to provide a peaceful, comfortable
home environment in which to nurture the husband and the
children. If she works outside the home, it should not interfere
with her responsibilities as wife and mother. Her right to
maintenance (that it is the husband's responsibility to provide for
all financial support for the family) is mainly to free her in her
roles of giving birth, of breastfeeding, and of rearing the children.

❖As for raising children, I am the primary caretaker being
with them twenty–four hours a day. I'm mostly in charge

of education and discipline though the father does play a very active role in the children's care and education, etc.

❖The Qur'an teaches the child that he (or she) must honor and obey their parents unless they are told to do something that goes against Qur'anic teaching. They are taught in Islamic school to be obedient and to respect their mother. There will be a time when I am old when it will be their turn to take care of me. They are also told to kiss the hand of their mother, as I am the one who will ensure their entrance into paradise.

Islamic Training Emphasized

The women expressed their concern about child–rearing in several areas. They especially want to pass on to their children the values of the Islamic community and religion. Living in a non–Muslim country makes it a little more difficult, and they feel they must train their children carefully.

❖Since I have become Muslim, I am more concerned about what my child sees and hears, and how that affects her. I want to raise her to choose Islam for herself, not force it on her. Of course, while I am raising her, I am making decisions I feel are right. I am teaching her values that are rarely taught to the children today in this country. I think it is my obligation as a mother to raise the next generation of Muslims to be good Muslims, good daughters and sons, good sisters and brothers, good husbands and wives, and good mothers and fathers.

My husband is the male role model for my daughter. He is not her natural father, but she loves him almost as if he were, and he loves her almost as if she were his own. I feel that he wants to impart good values to her, and on the children we will have, insha'Allah. But I will be with them the majority of the time, so what they learn will come mostly from me. I do want him to be active in raising our children because I think they need active Muslim male role models. We need to give them love and kindness, and try to shape them gently so they will grow up knowing they are part of a loving Muslim family.

❖As Muslims we must raise and teach our children to the best of our knowledge and more. In Islam we are encouraged to seek knowledge. Everything that I do as a mom has something Islamic involved: teaching love, Qur'an, prayers, manners, cleanliness, etc. It really comes easy when you have Islam in your heart! There is more to child–rearing than I said, but all of my techniques come from Islam. My husband plays a big role in child–rearing—more than is to be expected from a dad working eight to five. I must be more than an example and do my very, very best to give the best care.

❖My husband and I try our best to raise our children by the tenets of Islam. It is very difficult, however, once the children reach school age. They are exposed to so much that we would rather them not know about at a young age. Alhamdulillah, however, we have two hijab–wearing daughters, so I don't feel we're doing so badly. I hope my children will always feel free to come to me for support with any Islamic question. In turn, I expect them to listen to any guidance I may offer.

Many of the women expressed that their parenting wasn't so much different than how they were reared except they are emphasizing the Islamic principles and training. They are very aware of and attentive to the influences in their children's lives and try to keep them from harmful influences even as they are guiding them toward an Islamic path.

❖My children are being raised very much as I was except I hope to home school them. As a child I was raised in a very tight family, restricted TV, lots of books, lots of camping, restricted friends and associations. Sunday was family only. My husband works 5 or 6 days a week, 12–14 hours a day. When he has time off, he plays with the children and often takes the three–year–old out for awhile to give me a break. I'm with them 24 hours so most of the education and discipline falls on me. We must raise our children to have a strong sense of self and self confidence. They must know Islam as based on principles, values, and logic not just halal, haram, and wajeb. We must help them find their best life's work and set them on the road to achieve it.

❖Though some of my child–rearing practices are family traditions from my childhood, even these are influenced by Islam. There is no way to separate one from the other. We must raise our children Islamically if we are to fulfill part of our obligations as Muslims such as teaching them how to pray and fast. My husband is very helpful but most of the time he is away from home. Therefore, much of the responsibility for teaching the children is on me. I expect my children to respect me as it says in the Qur'an and to obey me.

❖Islam has been my guide in raising my boys. They were born Muslim. They know, respect, and practice Islam. They pray five times a day just as I do. They study Islam with me on a weekly basis. Islam is our lifestyle. My husband is an equal partner. He wants to be an important part of their life and is. They have a great relationship. We have a strong family. There is no danger of problems of straying. Our boys are well–grounded in a time when gang violence and other peer pressures abound.

The parents tend to express a "tough love" policy by expecting the children to respect them and to respond. Discipline is extended but usually in a loving and guiding manner. Severe and harsh punishment is not reflected in the statements of these women, nor do they perceive harshness and abuse in discipline as Islamically acceptable. The following response gives an overview of the theory and practice of discipline as interpreted by one woman.

❖Parents must be loving and kind to their children. In Islam, the slapping, hitting, spanking, or shaking of children is prohibited. These are forms of abuse that Muslim parents must not use.

We have numerous traditions against abuse from the Prophet Muhammad (pbuh) and his holy family (pbut). Because of this, I have tried to verbally explain to our children if they misbehave and demonstrate to them the correct behavior. Children so young cannot be expected to do what is correct and cannot benefit from a spanking because they do not understand it—they only know that they are being hurt. If the child runs into the street, hold the child by the hand or pick them up and hold them in your arms. Take the child to a safer place and watch them so they do not do it again. Spanking will not deter the child. It will just make him or her angry and then they will become sneaky, trying to do things when the parents are not watching.

My husband discusses the events that sometimes occur and the actions of our children. He points out their mistakes in judgment because he loves them and wants them to learn how to do what is right whenever they are presented with a similar situation in the future. He wants them to learn that they are responsible not only for their actions but also for the consequences of actions. I also discuss problems with our children; however, the two of us never reprimand our child at the same time. If one of us is discussing, the other one will stay silent because we do not want to gang up on him. Then we hug him and comfort him, reminding him that criticism of his action was done in love and we want only the best for him; that he should learn from his mistake and must not repeat the behavior.

Of course, we forgive our children's mistakes and we do not keep talking about it over and over again. Parents should not constantly pick on their children. Children need to feel safe in their homes and not be nervous about everything they do. Some children may be more sensitive than others and cannot accept criticism very well. They may need extra praise for their achievements to assure them that their parents love them. Praise can boost their self–esteem and then they may become more confident about themselves and their abilities.

As parents, we only ask that our children have respect for us, other people, and themselves. If a child is disrespectful of another person, it can become a habit that is hard to break. Our children are young and cannot make adult decisions. My husband and I make decisions for them. For example, we decided that when our children are promoted to junior high school, we would teach our children at home and they do not have any choice about this. As their parents, we feel we know what is best for them. The public school system constantly exposes our children to talk of (or activity in) alcohol, drugs, sex, and violence. After three months of home school, our middle child told me that he was glad that he was in home school because he had remembered the bullying he endured on a daily basis by a classmate the year before.

We also encourage their physical well–being by scheduling thirty minutes of exercise every morning. They have thirty minutes of free time after lunch to play basketball, work on the computer, or read. After school they may play soccer in the backyard or ride their bicycles on our street. They choose what kind of snack to prepare and then they must clean up the kitchen before leaving. With each responsibility that they take on, our children make us glad that they are learning and growing to be independent.

Education for the children is a top priority, but it has to be in the right setting. Some have chosen to home school their children, others have the availability of an Islamic school, and some feel the public school setting is acceptable with the backup in values they give at home. The Islamic guidelines for education for children allows them to not start being "book" educated until after age six. But other training and education for life should be going on during the early formative years.

❖My child–rearing techniques are to instill family values and Islamic values into my children and if that means living in a closed situation (no public school, neighborhood friends) then so be it. Muslim children do not require formal education until age six or seven where they are required to sit and learn. I will not put them into a school of this type until then. I am not against exploring Western child psychology methods for behavior and learning, but they should correspond with Islamic ideas.

My husband helps with the children and stays with them when I am working or in class. He is interested in the children's upbringing, is very loving and kind. He is also somewhat strict, too, and that is good.

Islamic schools are private schools and tuition is charged to help meet costs. In addition to tuition, transportation to and from school becomes a concern to parents and involves many miles of travel. Those who are able to arrange for Islamic schools for their children seemed very satisfied and very supported. Arabic, which is the religious language of Muslims, is taught as well as good discipline with kindness, the Qur'an, how to wear hijab, and the practices and obligations of Islam. Children in Islamic schools also build friendships with other Muslims their age and learn a peer standard that is different from that in the public schools.

❖Of course being Muslim has influenced the way we raise our children. My kids go to Islamic school even though I have to drive 15 miles to get them there. My husband is at home so he is very involved. My kids know that they owe me great respect and that paradise is under the feet of the mother. My obligation is to care for them and to raise them to be the best Muslims.

❖We follow Islamic principles so our child–rearing techniques are completely influenced by Islam. Again, we have the Islamic school to thank because we have support from them. My husband is very involved in child care. He likes spending time with the kids and that gives me a break. Also he likes spending time with me, so sometimes the kids go to a babysitter (a Muslim friend).

An alternative to attending an Islamic school is home schooling. This is working very well in some families where the mother is home and has the expertise and patience to do so. Sometimes the mothers share in the responsibility of teaching each other's children. A support group of and for parents of full–time and part–time home–educated Muslim children, The Islamic Home School Association of North America (IHSANA), assists by producing a newsletter.

❖In Islam, the raising of children is one of the most important things. Rearing one's children is the best possible way to bring a person closer to God. The first thing is to respect your child and his/her opinions even though it may be difficult. Because we want our children to grow up being good Muslims, we keep them away from negative influences as much as possible. In our case we decided public schools with the peer pressure and other negative teachings was not an option for us. Instead we home school. I do want them to have the freedom of friends so I let them meet American children (non–Muslim) but if I see anything negative, I pull them back and involve them in other activities.

The father of the children takes an active part in child rearing. He is involved in education with them—Islamic teachings, Qur'an, prayer, Islamic stories. He spends much of his free time with them. Raising children in any society takes a commitment from both mother and father.

❖Because of "negative" influence from the outside world, my husband didn't want the children to go to public school. This forced me to find an alternative, which existed in home schooling. Most of the child–rearing is my responsibility. He helps when he is asked, but not on a self–initiated "wanting to spend time with them" level.

My obligation is to discipline them toward one model, the Prophet Muhammad, and my right is to expect their submission and cooperation in this. Their rights are to expect shelter, food, clothing, and education; their obligation is to make this chore enjoyable to give, for them to be thankful for what they receive.

❖How I raise my child is very much influenced by being Muslim. I'm more cognizant of the satanic influences that come from all sides and, therefore, as of six months ago, we have no television. I've taught him in home school since he was in second grade and plan to continue.

My husband is as involved as he can be. He helps when he's not working. Having a big extended family around (seven adults) also helps. My child is to obey me and remember God. He has chores and duties around the home. I am to provide love, food, clothing, teaching, and a balance of play to his life to give him as much God–conscience and Islam as I can.

Only one of the women commented about the experience of having a child in public school even though the objective part of the questionnaire indicated that 47 percent of the families had children in public school. Sometimes only one of the children in the family attended public school, and it varied as to whether the students attended public school in high school or elementary. There were also those who sent their children to private schools that were not Islamic.

❖Both my husband and I are trying to raise our children to be good followers of Islam. We take our girls to tafseer classes and do a lot of things with our Muslim friends. We try to provide good role models for the children, believing it is important to keep them close to us and thus close to the faith. We also encourage outside activities like preschool and gymnastics so they will not feel isolated. We will provide alternative activities throughout their "growing–up" years so they will not feel alienated when not allowed to participate in activities at school which we feel are inappropriate for Muslims (eg. Christmas concerts, dances, mixed slumber parties, etc.). We believe it is possible to raise faithful followers of Islam in public schools for we have seen success stories firsthand, but we will seek alternative education routes if severe problems arise.

Parents Mutually Involved

The surveys indicated that both parents were involved in the care and training of the children. Reference was made to rights of children and parents from the aspect of rights that need to be extended to the children by the parents and from the children to the parents. They feel children's rights do not include having everything they may impulsively want. Children do have the right to be directed in the prescribed way through good parental guidance and have the right to safety, good care, and treatment that helps them maintain good self–esteem. On the other hand, parents have the right to receive respect and care from the children. Inherent in those guidelines for rights are respect, hard work, and a sense of authority that is often hard to maintain in our democratic setting where the children tend to claim their "rights" early on regarding what they want to do.

❖A hadith [one of the sayings, deeds, and practices of Prophet Muhammad] says the first school is the lap of the mother. The only thing that has changed since my conversion is my awareness of my children's rights. It was easy to quiet them before but they have a right to be heard. It was easy to smack their buttocks before, but is the smack justified? You can't leave marks or scars inside or out. I must constantly be aware of their rights and my responsibility toward them, to feed, clothe, and educate them both academically and religiously. One day, I'll have to answer for all of it.

❖Our child–rearing techniques are conservative and strict with *lots of love, hugs, and kisses*. My husband has always participated in all child–rearing activities. My rights with the children are equal to that of my husband, if not a little extra on my side. My obligations are to provide them the environment, rules, and love that they will need to grow

into compassionate, well–rounded adults with a clear view
of right and wrong. Their rights and obligations to me are
to treat me with respect.

As previously stated, the fathers are often very much involved
in the care of the children whether or not the wife works outside
the home or is involved in furthering her education. The fathers
may feel especially strong needs to be involved in the guidance of
their children when they are not living in a country that offers
support to their Islamic principles. Lacking the presence of
extended family may also foster a greater involvement with their
children. Specific reasons for the active involvement by the fathers
are not made clear in the responses of the women. The women do,
however, seem to appreciate their husband's involvement in child
care and training.

❖I am more concerned about what our children learn and
who teaches them than I would be if I weren't a Muslim.
My husband is very involved by spending time with them
in the evenings, playing with them, reading to them, and
teaching them things. He helps feed them and with potty
training and sometimes gives them a bath. He takes our
son with him sometimes when he has to go out, to spend
more time with him and to give me a break. I am about 95
percent of the time obligated to take care of their every
need. I am allowed to do anything within reason with
them. I always have my husband's permission to take them
with me wherever I go.

❖From day one, my husband has been very active and
helpful with the child–rearing. He has been watching our
daughter for several years while I worked outside the
home. He has never hit her or spanked her, and plays with
her often. I often feel he has high expectations—

sometimes not within reason in regards to dress, etc. Then we talk and obtain resolution.

❖My child–rearing techniques have not been influenced by being Muslim. I was already doing most of what I do before I converted. My level of patience and understanding in dealing with the children has improved, but I have not made any changes in the techniques. My husband is involved in caring for the children as much as he can be. When he is home we share the tasks just about equally. He bathes the children every other night, helps with hand washing and tooth brushing; deals with arguments, fixes snacks, and occasionally reads for our nightly story time. My children are young (six and four). Our rights and obligations with respect to each other are still very basic.

The responses of the women to their responsibility of child–rearing reflected how seriously they perceived that role. They yearn to provide the kind of training and opportunities that will result in their child becoming an adult who will be in submission to Allah and be good, practicing Muslims. Those of us who have raised children in our own religious traditions have yearned for our skills to be adequate to the task of rearing children in the path that would lead them to God. How similar are our desires!

9. Respecting Divergent Paths
Working Together to Build and Maintain Relationships

Jodi's different lifestyle and dress were difficult for our whole family at first. Jodi's uncle, not many years older than she and always close to the family, made what he thought was a funny statement about her scarf in front of a visitor, and it hurt Jodi terribly. Yet he was the one who had dreams of Jodi being in danger and his being the one to rescue her. Her cousin, who had been a best friend growing up, no longer understood how to relate to her in this new lifestyle. Her grandma could not understand her choice that resulted in such changes, but Grandma, being basically kind and accepting, was able to deal with the situation in a loving way. There were stresses with other family members, but as time went by it all became easier. We are so grateful for the time and close proximity that we have had over the years to work through the various relational changes. Jodi and Reza certainly did their part too. They have had to decide where they could give, what was important to them, and how they could retain their commitment while maintaining family relationships.

❖ ❖ ❖

Each person (and each family) needs to define who he or she is, what they believe, and what values are important. This is an essential part of the growing up process for all people, regardless of culture. Therefore a wide diversity of beliefs and practices can exist within a family, a nation, or a religious system.

The Islamic world covers many countries, cultures, and ethnic peoples. What is the norm in one culture may not even exist in another Islamic area. There are five types of activity: (1) obligatory (2) encouraged (3) legal or halal (4) cautionary, and (5) forbidden. The obligatory and forbidden acts are universal and should be practiced in all Islamic areas. Examples of obligatory acts would be the daily prayers and the fasting at Ramadan. Forbidden acts would be activities such as consuming alcohol, cheating, lying, and eating pork. The other three, encouraged (or highly important), the legal (halal), or the cautionary fall in the category of personal choice. These would include doing extra prayers, getting married and having children, doing good deeds, or being cautious about behaviors such as gossip. There are many guidelines for living, and these may be highly influenced by one's particular community of Muslims, the school of Muslim thought one follows, or the traditions of the husband's country of origin.

American women converts are trying to combine who they have been in the past and their habits with the practices of Islam. The divergent path these daughters have chosen cause traditional relations to be changed. Social habits between Muslims and non–Muslims are different, belief systems may clash, and both the families of origin and the daughters will be called on to reestablish new ways to relate to each other. There are some guidelines that we can keep in mind as we relate to Muslims in the workplace, in the family, in public places, and as friends and acquaintances.

Food and Drink Considerations

Pork products and alcoholic drinks are considered haram (forbidden) by practicing Muslims. They check labels carefully to be sure those products are not in food items they purchase.

Many practicing Muslims also try to eat only halal (approved) meats that are slaughtered in a prescribed manner. These meats are purchased at specialty stores, or the families butcher their own meat in the appropriate manner.

Checking with the Muslim family is the only way to determine what is best to serve when they come to visit. Vegetarian meals or fish are acceptable alternatives, or they may bring an halal main entree to be served along with what is being prepared. Some of the women expressed concern about eating when visiting families.

❖Stress usually comes up when we visit my parents. Since we eat only Muslim slaughtered halal meats, we are reluctant to eat anything, so we would bring our own food. Even though we have explained the Islamic method of slaughter, I feel that they are uncomfortable with us bringing our own food. They thought this was another rejection, as if their food was not good enough for us or was unclean. However, when they come to visit in our home, they eat whatever I cook and we seem to have a much happier and less stressful time.

❖I would *never* leave my child with my parents. There is too much pork in the house.

❖The worst thing about visiting my folks is eating. They don't care what they eat. My parents sometimes get mad when I tell them I can't eat the same food they are eating.

❖I do not leave my children with my family. We have never visited for more than a couple of hours at a time since I became Muslim. In doing this, I also avoid another potential problem—that of halal food. My parents do not understand or accept the concept of halal/haram food. We simply avoid the issue and don't eat at their house.

Alcohol is offensive to most Muslims and they would feel more comfortable if it is not served when they are present. They may even avoid restaurants that have a bar or serve liquor. They may often avoid business lunches or company picnics where alcohol is served.

Modesty in Dress and Social Relationships

Many Muslims try to avoid places or media that feature scantily clad persons or actions that are considered offensive. Even family swimming pools may be off limits. The woman may be dressing hijab and covering her hair by way of normal practice when in the presence of men other than her father, husband, sons, or brothers. She will appreciate the family's help in providing a chance for her to cover if other male company drops by.

It is also important to be aware of the type of television programs viewed when Muslim children are present. Some of the children's shows most American kids watch may not be considered appropriate for children by the Muslim mom and dad. Non–Muslims should find out what is allowable if the children are involved; even many Muslim adults don't allow themselves to watch everything that is on. Scenes that show dating relationships, dancing, or scantily clad women are common ones to avoid.

❖Islamically, I don't like for the children to watch commercials or dancing, rap music, dating situations, looseness on TV, anything which you can see by turning it on for two minutes or less. I would prefer they not get used to musical instruments or music which has adult rock –and–roll rhythm even if it has children's lyrics. My parents are pretty good about avoiding these things.

There are also guidelines for male/female relating. Males do not shake hands with females and often will not look directly at them. Men should not reach out to touch Muslim women or be too openly curious or friendly. One should be reticent but pleasant. Usually, the safe approach is for the men to talk with men and the women to talk with women. Women will often greet other women with a cheek–to–cheek greeting.

Celebrating the Holidays and Gift Giving

American holidays may be very difficult for the families of origin of the Muslim converts and for Muslims in general. Office parties featuring alcohol, dancing, and/or flirting relationships; the giving of gifts such as liquor, hams, turkeys; national or Christian religious ceremonies and decorations—all these are unacceptable to Muslims. Avoidance of holiday celebrations may be the behavioral norm for Muslims in the business world.

For the families, holiday times have been worked out in a variety of ways. Some of the women respondents refused to be part of the traditional Western celebrations at all. Others have modified the celebrations in order to be with the family. Still others participate in almost the same way as before.

❖My children have the best of both religions. My parents and in–laws make a big deal about Christmas. We accept their gifts and explain the concept to our boys. They don't serve us pork or alcoholic beverages. My family is my life. No problems. Lots of love—always was!

Thanksgiving seems to be one holiday that can most easily be worked through if halal meat or an alternative is served. Attitudes toward participation may change as the couple have children, and the Muslims may feel a need to withdraw from holidays they are now celebrating that reflect non–Muslim religious holidays or even national holidays. Birthdays may not be celebrated in the same way as non–Muslims and activities may need to be negotiated.

Muslim holidays are of great importance to the Muslims, and they celebrate with great commitment. Eid al–Fitr, the most important celebration of the year, is on the first day after the month of Ramadan (the month of fasting). Gifts are sometimes given, cards are sent, and families of origin may be included if it is convenient and families are willing. This inclusion seems to be an exception, however, for Eid is most often celebrated with other Muslims. The women have found many problems with celebrating Christian or national holidays with their birth families and have had to determine the extent to which they were willing to be with the family at such times.

❖I try to avoid talking about the "holidays." My brother and sisters understand that I don't celebrate them, and they respect me for it. But my parents don't understand and keep asking every year if I'm coming over for the holidays and what to do with the presents they got for me, my husband, and kids.

❖My father's mother was ill when he was young, and his father was an alcoholic. My mother's birth mom abandoned her at two years of age. So my parents always tried to do special things during the holidays with my brother and me (we were the only family they felt they had). My not celebrating Christmas any longer was especially hard for them. We accommodated their feelings with much compromise on their part. They may buy our children Christmas gifts and the children may only open them after we read and recite passages from the Qur'an regarding Jesus' birth, Mary, the Mother of Jesus and command-ments about what to believe in the Qur'an.

Thanksgiving is enjoyed with halal (Islamically al-lowed) turkey killed in the prescribed manner but no baked ham. We've basically turned it into a good excuse to eat together! My parents agree that is most important. It helps establish and maintain family bonds and memories.

My mom, dad, and brother get anxious for Eid gifts which now take the place of Christmas gifts. I really try to emphasize the Islamic holidays for the sake of my children. I do get a lot of competition with my mom and Christmas, so I have to emphasize Islamic holidays more than most.

✤My family doesn't really follow Christmas as a Christian holiday (not as Christ's birthday), but since everybody usually has Christmas off and many brothers and sisters have married those who do practice, we now have a family dinner and some exchange gifts.

✤I would like to include my family more in our Islamic celebrations. But many times that means traveling two or three hours to where other Muslims gather. There have not been that many chances. Often the main part of celebration is a special congregational prayer, which they would not participate in anyway, since they are not Muslim.

✤I send Eid cards and candy to my nieces and nephews.

✤Last Eid was the first time I gave presents to my family in exchange for the presents they gave us at Christmas.

✤For my Islamic holidays, Eid al–Fitr and Eid al–Adha, I send my mom Eid cards that are homemade. And I will put such things as: Hadith—Heaven lies below the mother's feet, etc. I invite them to eat at the park or at the mosque during the Islamic holidays. My mom and my sister do come to see what it is like.

✤Because they live in another state, my family has never participated in any of our Islamic celebrations. They keep their distance, and we each allow the other to be as we are. I call some of my relatives on the telephone, and I send letters or cards at Thanksgiving and Christmas.

Sometimes if I cannot reach them on Christmas, I call them and wish them a Happy New Year on the first day of January.

❖When we first got married, we went for Christmas and exchanged gifts. But this year we have a child, and we need to get them used to the idea of our not being involved in Christmas. My parents sent us gifts this year and we thanked them, but we didn't give them any. And we didn't send out cards. We do plan on celebrating Eid, and we are going to send them a card to explain what we do. Hopefully it won't be an issue by the time our daughter is older. I do want her to know my side of the family, so we will have to work on how to do that.

❖I think that for my family of origin the main point of stress was probably Christmas—whether it's okay to give us gifts, include us for dinner, etc. It took a lot of time and talk to come to terms with Christmas because I cannot turn my back on my family of origin. My husband and I joined my family for dinner and received gifts from them with the understanding that this is a celebration in which we do not participate and that we wouldn't be reciprocating the gift exchange. We will, however, reciprocate by including my family in our Islamic celebrations. Everyone was in agreement with this idea and the spirit of the "season" was not dampened.

❖My family doesn't show any interest in our Islamic holidays. I tell them about them a few weeks or a month ahead of time, but they don't seem to care, and I think they avoid being around us during that time.

Gift giving goes along with holiday and birthday times. Being open to discussions on how these occasions could be observed helps preserve the joy of sharing as a family or in the office setting. Creating some new traditions that respect each other's feelings might make the occasion more special than ever.

Parents (or other relatives) may find it best to forego giving Muslims presents on non–Muslim holidays, choosing instead to give gifts at other times, either on their holidays or just for the sake of giving. One could also find out when Eid is and ask about sending gifts then, checking to see what gifts are appropriate. American toys such as Batman, the Turtles, Power Rangers, or Barbie and Ken may be completely off–limits. Even clothes with Thomas the Tank Engine or bed sheets with Barney may not be acceptable. If parents talk it over with their daughter, they will probably discover she has some good ideas. Then if parents want to give gifts, they can follow the guidelines agreed on and do it with joy.

❖They know we are Muslim and that we don't celebrate Christian holidays the same way they do. My mother sometimes sends gifts to our children for no particular reason—just because she sees something they might like. She also sends gifts at Christmas time. We accept them as gifts for the New Year. We celebrate Jesus' birth, may God's peace be upon him, with a prayer.

My family of origin lives far from us and have very little understanding of Islam and the Eid holidays. So far, they have not been included in our Islamic celebrations, but if they lived closer to us they would be included as much as they would like to be.

❖My sisters and parents (father and stepmother) are sensitive to the fact that we don't celebrate Christian holidays. They always ask before giving or doing anything which could be construed to be related to such holidays. They respect our holidays. I have no concerns about the children with them. It helps that we have a varied family encompassing many types of religions: Christian, Jewish, Buddhist, and Muslim. It is an unspoken family rule to respect others' beliefs so long as they aren't harming themselves or others. Both my parents' families do this.

Leaving the Children in the Care of Others

Some Muslim parents are willing to let the children stay with the grandparents or others for a few hours or overnight, but it isn't often. Muslim parents feel very responsible and have so many things they want controlled in their children's environment that those outside the Muslim family almost have to prove themselves. This is true of extended family members or even with non–Muslim neighborhood children. Careful consideration is even given when leaving children in the care of other Muslims.

It is best to listen to the concerns of the parents and try to follow the rules. Such ordinary things as bathroom habits require different learning by non–Muslims. Being supportive of Muslim religious views with the children and refraining from "indoctrinating" with opposing views will be much appreciated by the parents. Care should be taken about the television programs or music that is played in their presence. Providing the right food and omitting the forbidden foods is also important.

❖My parents often request for the children to sleep over. The children and others have noticed my mom asking the children if they have prayed and reminding them to do so. (Appropriate if done from Islamic viewpoint!) My area of concern is my ten–year–old daughter. Mom thinks she is too young to worry about modest dress and buys her mini–skirts, which I hurriedly hide away. My daughter does not wear hijab yet, but she is accepting of the idea and very positive about it. She does dress modestly outside the house mostly in cotton printed long sleeves, loose fitting pants or a long skirt.

❖I visit my family on a regular basis. I let my mother watch the children for three to four hours, but with other grandchildren at my mother's it is hard for me to leave them. I worry more about my children picking up non–Islamic ideas more from peers than from adults (e.g., when nieces play Barbies they usually have Ken and Barbie dating). The cousins also have boyfriends or girlfriends at school that they talk about.

❖My children will always be welcome at my parents, and my mother is wonderful with the kids.

❖My family knows they do not have to change to accept me the way I am now. My child gets no different treatment than any other child except they know he can't have beer, pork, or any foods that we don't allow.

❖During the summer my brothers would always let their children spend a week or two with my parents, but our children never went to visit their grandparents without my husband and me. They never tried to push us or persuade us because they knew our children could not eat their food.

❖I know if we left our little girl alone with my mom when she is older, she would try to Christianize her, and that I *cannot* abide by! The fact that I can't trust her causes me great sadness—the depth of which my husband cannot understand. I must abandon my mother for her own stubbornness but this I do, not only for the good of my marriage and family but for my own good as well.

❖Leaving my child is difficult in that they feed him too much junk food and spoil him, which I know is usual for grands. The biggest concern is him not eating anything but halal meat, so they get upset when he can only eat fish and vegetarian meals.

❖My parents have assured me that if, God forbid, something should happen to my husband and me, they would make sure our children would be raised Muslim and keep close with my husband's family. Both his and my family have mutual concern and respect for each other.

The Daily Prayers

Often in the fervent discussion regarding school prayer, no consideration is given to those who may be of a religious faith other than Christian. Muslim youth are brought up to pray five times a day with at least two of those times during the school day. Yet any consideration to providing for their needs for a place and time to pray is probably avoided in most discussions on school prayer.

This also becomes a problem for those Muslims in the business world who need to have both place and time scheduled to allow them the privacy for a few minutes, probably twice a day, to perform this obligatory practice.

When they visit us, Jodi and Reza feel free to go into another room of the house that isn't being used when it is time for their prayers. If non–Muslim parents are uncomfortable with this practice, an agreement should be worked out with all parties involved.

❖My parents are very considerate of our beliefs. They have no problems with us praying at their house, are extremely careful of what they fix us to eat, and try not to say anything offensive.

Muslims may feel very uncomfortable when prayers are offered in the name of Jesus Christ and try to avoid situations where this may occur.

❖I am grateful that my parents understand our feelings of being in offense if we are present when a prayer is given in the name of Jesus. They are careful to close their prayers "In the name of our Mutual God, Amen."

Religious and Political Discussions

I have found that Muslims are very certain about what they believe. They feel they have the truth, and they can't understand why non–Muslims don't see it. As with all people, a variety of opinions and interpretations also exists among Muslims, and political or religious discussions can become quite animated whether between Muslims or between Muslims and non–Muslims.

One day after I got into either a religious or political discussion with Reza and Jodi, I started to cry. It was just too much for me. "Jodi," I said, "we just can't talk about this topic anymore—it hurts me too much."

Jodi said, "Oh, Mom, we can't do that; we have to talk about it."

Reza gave us these words of wisdom: "Sometimes, even in my own family, we find things that we can't talk about, and we just have to be together because we love each other."

And that has been good advice for us many times. Oh, we try to talk, and Jodi and Reza know just about how far they can push me before I get upset—then they back off. Their beliefs mean so much to them that they want to share them and yet it often sets up explosive situations for family and acquaintances.

❖I love my parents dearly and respect them to the utmost extent. I just wish they would ask me what I believe or just read a bit of the Qur'an. Of course I would like to see them embrace Islam, but at this point or anytime in the near future it is not realistic.

❖When I am visiting my family I feel as though I'm surrounded by idols, but since they accept my Islam I tolerate their beliefs also.

❖I hope to just keep things going as is and keep in touch with my parents, especially since we have a baby now. They are my parents and I should care for them. Everything seems to be a point of stress for our family. It is difficult to talk about anything except the weather, the car we're thinking about buying, what vacation we'll take next summer.

The women's responses on the questionnaire indicate there are a variety of ways to work things out with the family of origin. There are also those families not as open as others. There is a difference in how far and how open some can go. Although questions on the survey were not directed toward relationships in the business world, I have, in my own conversations with Muslims often picked up their frustrations connected with social relationships, holidays, lack of understanding, and the feelings of prejudice toward them.

The stories seem to illustrate that many times the more cooperative and supportive the family or acquaintances are, the less conservative the women feel they have to be. A more strict attitude may be a protective response to lack of support and trust.

10. The Daughters Speak Out
What the Muslim Converts Would Like Us to Know

Twelve years had passed since Jodi had chosen to become Muslim. The healing had taken years, but I found myself okay with Jodi as Muslim. There are still twinges of regret at times when I see that choice blocking some things we could do together either as mother and daughter or as grandparents and grandchildren. But my respect is there for her and that which her life demonstrates as good and upstanding.

I found myself wanting to know more about other women who had converted. How had their families accepted it? Were the daughters able to work it through with their birth families? Could my story help them move toward healing? I really wanted to assist other grieving parents in their acceptance of these daughters and the path they had chosen.

My decision to do something to share with others about the strength and goodness I saw in my daughter's lifestyle and that of her Muslim friends was made one Sunday morning while I was still in bed. I remember swinging my feet out of bed onto the floor and as I got up, it was as if I were taking the first steps toward a new and challenging endeavor.

I talked with Jodi about my ideas. She was in the beginning courses of an M.S. degree in nursing, had two young children, and worked part–time. I'm sure she wasn't eager to take on any other responsibilities, but she agreed to invite to her home a few

American–born Muslim women to talk about the possibilities. If this was something these women felt was important, I would go ahead with the project.

Only two women came to meet with us, but it was through their support, encouragement, and ideas for proceeding that I felt the determination and enthusiasm to carry out the almost three–year project of gathering information from other American–born Muslim women, writing my own story, and then finding a way to share it. At this first meeting, the Muslim converts discussed how important it was to them to help family members understand better what they had chosen, how and what they were doing, and how they longed for acceptance by their families. They also wanted to share with the population in general what it means to them to be Muslim.

I have learned so much from these women. I am grateful to them for sharing their lives with me through the questionnaire. This project has smoothed over the scars that I didn't even know were there. *Daughters of Another Path* has been further healing for me, and I salute these women who have the strength to walk in such a path. Not many of us could do it.

❖ ❖ ❖

Through the questionnaires, the women shared their stories about their conversion, their joys and struggles in taking on the Muslim practices, and how they relate with families of origin, husbands and in–laws, their children, and the world of work. The last question to which they responded on the questionnaire was: "What would you like the American public to know about you that has not yet been asked?" What would they say to us? This is what they wrote. Let us hear them.

Who We Are

❖I would like the American public to know that we are people just like them. We struggle to pay bills (we don't all have oil wealth), we worry about tomorrow, we want peace. We just happen to have strong religious convictions and try to live our life to be acceptable to Allah. My husband didn't make me dress this way, and I'm not oppressed. I'm set free—free from the bondage of fashion, clothes, hair, shoes, and the like. Inheritance is guaranteed to me and my children after payment of debts. I don't hate America or Americans. I still love Jesus, and pray to the same one God he referred to. I don't hate Jews or Israel. In fact, I would love to live there if I knew I wouldn't be persecuted. What I do hate is injustice, lies, ungodliness, prejudice, abortion, defiling of flesh, and all disobedience to the commandments of God, because I love God.

❖I have chosen this way because I like it. I have not given up anything that I didn't want to give up. I have not been brainwashed. I am an educated person with full–thinking capabilities. I am not a traitor to my country but an advocate of the world. I will always be Muslim with or without my husband. I did not become Muslim because I "love" my husband. I do want my children to grow up Muslim. I do expect them to be Muslim and my daughter to wear hijab. Everyone is always asking me these things. I will put my children in an Islamic environment, not a non–Islamic environment, then ask them to be Muslim.

❖The average Muslim seeks peace. All that one hears about are the Muslim extremists, the political revolutionaries. These are a minority. The majority (by the way, Arabs only comprise one–fifth of the Islamic world) are peaceful. Look at the Indonesians we never hear about, and their numbers are far greater than the Arabs.

❖I am willing to communicate with them and answer questions if they are respectful of my opinions and beliefs.

❖I became a Muslim of my own free will.
I am a person with my own mind.
I study the facts before I commit to something.
Islam is the best choice I could ever make.
I am happy being a Muslim woman.
It is very hard to communicate with your family after such a big and complete change.

    I would like to encourage parents of Muslim converts to ask their children why they changed and try to understand them. It's not easy to live in this society after becoming a Muslim. You see things and people differently, and they see you as different, too. It helps a whole lot if you know that your family is at least talking to you about it and trying to comprehend what you are going through and how important this change is to you. We are changing for the better, for the sake of Allah.

❖The only thing I feel Americans need to know is that if a person or a woman converts to Islam, that it is not because we are being forced into it. No one can force another person to pray, learn Arabic, to put on long sleeves, dresses, cover the hair, or any other practice that a Muslim must do. We are Americans. We have rights just like anyone else to work and to support what we believe in.

❖I would like to remind the American public that I am a human being just like them. I do not like to be ridiculed. I feel sad when someone mocks the clothing I wear. Would you mock a Christian nun for wearing her habit or an Amish or Mennonite woman for wearing her bonnet?

    I have not been brainwashed by my husband. I am an intelligent person who chose to become a Muslim. Islam is founded on the precept that there is no force in religion. You can believe your way and I need to believe my way.

Some people who want to discredit Islam suggest that women are treated like second–class citizens or as inferior to men. They say that Muslim women must feed the men and children first and only eat what is left. This is a gross distortion of the truth. Yes, sometimes women eat later than others do, but it is not a punishment or a sentence imposed on her because she is a woman. When a woman feeds others first, she is doing so because of her love and concern. She knows that children need to eat often to stay healthy and grow normally. She understands that men need to eat to maintain their strength so they can go to work or to school. She makes sure that women who are pregnant drink their milk, eat plenty of fruits and vegetables, and take their vitamins. She feels that she cannot eat and satisfy her own hunger if others need something.

Muslims do not celebrate Christmas, but we hope that our relatives, neighbors, and co–workers who are Christian have a wonderful holiday. Please do not think that our children are deprived because we do not put up a Christmas tree or decorations. We have other holidays that you are not aware of, and we think our children are happy and growing up just fine.

❖I am not oppressed, and it is not degrading to wear proper clothing. I'd like them to know that my husband does the laundry, helps with cleaning (even does the toilet bowl!) and helps look after the children so I can go out. How about the so called liberated woman? Muslim women do not change their name when married. We are not supposed to take our husband's last name. When, insha' Allah, my daughter is married, her name will remain as she is recognized as an individual, an equal human being. No need for hyphens.

❖Not all Muslims in America are either foreigners or African–Americans. There are many white–American Muslims in the country. A lot of people find it hard to believe that you can be white and American and a Muslim at the same time. We have more rights than Christian women or any other women.

❖As you can tell, I'm a little different because I feel that the spiritual aspects of my faith are very important, possibly more than the day–to–day problems of what to wear, what to eat, etc. My faith is very deep, however, and will not waver. Something else about me is that I was diagnosed with Non-Hodgkin's Lymphoma over six years ago. I've had one round of chemo and have not needed treatment for five years. I had both my children (five years and fifteen months) after having cancer. My life is very interesting but also difficult with this extra problem thrown in. My faith in God has helped me immensely though this time, and I firmly believe that getting cancer was God's will for me. I am grateful because it has taught me so much: to live now, to love myself and my family, to worry only about big things — "Don't sweat the small stuff"— and it turned my life around to where I'm much more assertive and outspoken than I used to be. But that's a whole other book in itself.

❖Don't judge me by the few Muslims who do un–Islamic things in the name of Islam. Get to know me, talk to me, invite me to your schools and churches, and let's allow ourselves to dialogue about each other's religion. Don't be afraid of Islam. Get to know me. Ask us what books best describe Islam instead of the paper or anti–Islamic books written by "Middle East experts." Don't think I am repressed by my clothes. When you look at me, look at

Abraham's wife and Jesus' mother and how they are dressed. It is nothing new. It is part of your heritage.

❖I have mixed feelings. I do public speaking on Islam. I tell people we are just like them. We have our dreams and goals and love our families, but some of our attitudes and approaches to problem–solving are different. We are not oppressed or repressed by our faith, but only by ourselves. We are as are all people—good and bad. Americans and Europeans must be careful because those governments have an agenda that is definitely anti–Muslim (our own Congress passed a resolution in the mid '80s declaring Islam to be the greatest danger to the U.S.). They must filter what they are told and seek truth. We Muslims must stop hiding and making excuses and speak for ourselves. In many ways, we represent the positive and often imaginary values which founded this nation but with some very positive differences. As Muslims we need to clean our own closets, shake ourselves up, and re–examine what we are passing off as Islam before we start knocking on anyone's door to tell them about it.

❖[From new single convert in her 40s with a teenage daughter] Being Muslim is the best and the hardest thing in my life. It is all the answers and all the tools. I was fired from my job on February 28, 1994. I am filing a claim with the Ohio Civil Rights Commission because I feel my termination was due to my reversion [sometimes this word is used in place of "conversion"] to Islam. With every struggle comes ease. The Qur'an is an infinite source of answers, counsel, and warning. I am grateful to Allah for these struggles, yet as a weak human I continue to vacillate between joy 80 percent of the time and something less positive 20 percent of the time. The greatest blessings for me in Allah include my reliance on Allah, my loss of my previously short temper (it's gone!), learned patience, and the peace and tranquility reflected by my Muslim name which means for all of us, Allah is there, Allah is there. The greatest difficulty is to give up old habits of trying to control my life, a need to understand, and to accept the fact that although Islam is perfect, Muslims are not.

❖I am not a foreigner. I am not an alien. I expect them to treat me and my family with the respect that we deserve. I wish the culture and government of this country could have a system for a standard of living that would allow a Muslim family to live without going into debt or welfare.

❖I want people to know that I don't worship cows, that I don't get oppressed because of Islam, that Islam frees women, that I worship the same God as Christians and Jews, and that Muslims are not all terrorists! I wish people would open their minds and stop being so ignorant. Stop staring and laughing at women who wear hijab! It's their right and their husbands/fathers aren't forcing them to do so! Accept us as Americans, and live and let live!

❖We are not stupid and we are here to serve Allah (SWT) first and not our men. Our duty is this life, and we are happy with our choice.

❖Just because I cover my head does not make me a weirdo, a fundamentalist, a suppressed woman, or a weak woman. I hate it that everywhere I go people stare (sometimes with mean looks). I just want to be left alone to live my life as I want.

❖One of the biggest misconceptions is that all Muslims are from the Middle East or are married to someone from this region. This is not the case. There are thousands of

American Muslims who learned about Islam from other Americans. Both my husband and I are examples of this fact.

❖The best thing that ever happened to me in my life was becoming Muslim. Although my religious and political views may differ from many Americans, I would hope that they would be open–minded enough to know that "different" doesn't always equal "bad." Muslim women (who are granted their rights under Islam) are not chained to their houses or beaten regularly or tortured. We are part of society, and have a most important task. As Imam Ali said, "Nations are raised on the laps of mothers." We have a very important job to do. I would hope that the American public would not belittle that job.

What Islam Is About

❖Americans need to understand that Muslims are just living their lives by how they feel Allah (SWT) wants us to live. We are a very misunderstood religion. We are also the most growing religion in the world. In ten years we will, insha'Allah, be the second largest religion in the United States. Why are Americans turning from Christianity to Islam? Americans need to look past the stereotypes and look to the real Islam, the Islam of peace, the Islam which is getting more and more followers every day. Getting an Islamic society, to me, doesn't mean being fanatical or militant. It means having a society where the members are following the moral codes that Allah gave to us, as well as the religious obligations and social laws. Islam governs all of our lives. It is for all time, for all peoples. If Americans looked closely at Islam and realized that, then Islam would at last be understood.

❖Islam is not a prison for women as has been the belief in America for many years! It has sensible guidelines and laws as every decent society has, but Islam *is* flexible, where some others are "written in stone" and cannot be altered.

❖I would like the American public to realize that Muslim women are not second–class citizens. We don't walk behind our husbands, and we do have inalienable rights. Islam is not an extremist religion. Islam does not believe in extremes. Islam always promotes the middle road. Islam is not an Arab thing or an African–American thing; it is a religion for all peoples of all nationalities. Islam is a timeless religion that is suitable for all times and places. The beauty and antiquity of Islam has no bounds. In summary, Islam is a religion of peace and happiness.

❖If you ever saw what Islam really is, you would adore it immediately. As yet it is only an ideal in our minds!

The marriage relationship is protected and sexuality blossoms behind the veil! The streets would be safe. Your children would not be exposed to sex and drugs. They would receive a values education and practical skills.

Your husband's income would be enough to support the family, leaving you free to either work or have as many babies as you want, to study and grow in other ways.

People would not live in fear of unemployment or mortgage foreclosure. The economy would be based on small local businesses and an interest–free banking system. Life would be affordable again.

All that is only the beginning. If you could ever enter a beautiful, spacious mosque and participate in true prayer to God Most High, you would become truly satisfied and dignified. Some day all this will be ours by God's mercy.

❖Islam is a way of life! It has answers on every aspect of life. I choose Islam as my way of life by conviction—not by force or for my husband. I love my Islam and I feel that when I was born I was a Muslim and was raised Christian. Now I have reverted—not converted—to the true and straight path. I have achieved success. I've come back to Islam! May Allah always keep my heart pure and on the straight path.

❖As a Muslim woman I would like to say that Islam has liberated me in many ways. Most Americans see Muslim women as an oppressed lot, but I would like them to know that if Muslim women are oppressed, it's because they forsake the true Islam and follow their country's cultural practices. Islam throws away all the garbage that keeps women down and lifts them up to a status of self–respect and confidence.

Most American women feel that they are the most liberated women on earth, but they are not really relieved from the bonds of oppression. Anyone who has to have a perfect body for fear of rejection, anyone who has to reveal their bodies to receive so–called "attention," anyone who gets paid less for equal work versus a male counterpart, anyone in those categories is still oppressed, and the only solution is to throw the chains of bondage away and accept God and Islam in their life.

❖The American Muslim woman is not oppressed and our cover (hijab) is our right, not a punishment. We consider the Western way of life a step backward not forward. The Middle Eastern woman may see the so–called glamour of American Western lifestyle because their country practices culture and not Islam. If Islam was really practiced in the countries of my Eastern sisters, Western (females) would be fighting for Islamic rights.

✤The one most important issue I would like to get across, not only to the American public but even to many Muslims themselves, is that Islam must be judged on its own merits and not on the behavior of Muslims. Islam is a perfect system because it was created by God, just as we were. We, however, were not created perfect. We have free will and we choose our ways of life and make our own decisions; sometimes they are the correct decisions and sometimes they aren't. Also, I hope that non–Muslims will someday understand that every Muslim, true Muslim who lives by the laws of God, is a fundamentalist, and would understand the true meaning of that word. Regardless of the 1400+ years that have passed since the teachings of God through the Prophet Muhammad, Islam has not changed. In fact, the laws of God have never changed since Adam was created by God. God is not creating different humans than he did before. We are all human beings created by God. When we are born we have the same needs for love, affection, food, protection, and the same need to worship a higher being. These needs change as we mature and become shaped by our environment, but they remain essentially human needs. Change, however, never starts with countries, or leaders. It starts in the home, with the children, where the women rule. As soon as the Muslim women of the world realize this, the changes for the better will begin.

How We, As Muslims, Experience America

✤Americans in general seem to have a tendency to stereotype. They see us in a scarf and automatically think our husbands dominate us and that we are conservative.

✤This response will be the hardest because of the bitterness I feel toward this country. "The land of the free, home of the brave . . ." is nonexistent and the hypocrisy of this government really burns me up. The arrogance of this society that this is the best society and culture on earth in terms of women rights, human rights, children rights, minority rights is exasperating. The statement I make to people when they push their superiority on me is "This is America where everyone has a right to choose what they want to believe." Personally, I do not believe the American experiment is working. The society has been stripped of all values and Christian churches have warped the Bible so badly by giving people the philosophy that all sins will be forgiven and whatever feels good do it. I know that no society is perfect, but I want to increase my children's odds of success by putting them in an environment of a one–culture society, the culture and society with values that we hold important—a society with a limited amount of choices as to acceptable behavior. My husband and I can provide the high–tech opportunities of the West without poisoning our children with the value–deficient culture of the United States.

❖American women have chosen or accepted Islam through research and understanding and not by force or influence from their husbands. Just because there is a story of one crazy Iranian who abused his family—even if it is true—doesn't mean the whole country is like that. I urge people to think about what kinds of abuse and molestations go on here every second! I urge the American people to use their God–given brain and not to sleep through life!

❖It gives me great pain to know that Muslims and Islam are so terribly misunderstood by the majority of Americans, which gives rise to hatred, dirty looks, and rude comments, which impedes our rights as Americans to practice our religion freely. This country was founded by religious people seeking a country where they would not be persecuted for their beliefs. We are now even more of a melting pot than ever, and if we want to succeed as a nation and keep the ideals of the Constitution alive, we have to understand, accept and respect each other, regardless of religion, customs, or style of dress. I strongly encourage all Americans, whenever they see a woman in long, modest clothing covering all but her hands and face, instead of staring and feeling sorry for her, smile, greet her in peace, knowing that she is a strong, confident person trying to worship her God and your God the best she can. We are all citizens of this country where we are supposed to be free to worship as we please. Let's work together to keep it that way.

Epilogue

When Jodi came home to visit us that Thanksgiving day and shared the news with us of her conversion to Islam, it was like she had stabbed us with a knife. How could our sweet daughter do anything as bizarre as this? Both my husband, Joe, and myself were deeply hurt. Certainly, Jodi did not want to hurt us—but she had—and we were unable to understand what she had done. We were numb, but we were also angry and not sure we wanted our daughter as a part of our family. A decision would need to be made. Should we just consider she was no longer welcome in our home and treat her as if she were dead?

Jodi was not the first daughter who had disappointed her parents by making a decision contrary to their tradition. In fact, daughters and sons rarely make decisions that are completely in harmony with parental wishes. Oftentimes we have discovered the parental response is "get out and never come back; you are dead to our family." We were very fortunate that we were able to resist such a temptation. It could be worked out. As a family we would try to understand, and in trying to understand, we also have journeyed on another path and discovered a way of life which although strange to Americans, is wholesome and fulfilling for many of those who have chosen the Muslim experience.

Part of the discovery was that the media portrayal of Islam which is generally negative, does not often view the positive kinds of things that are happening. The negative sells. Therefore, the view most often displayed does not consider the wonderful, strong women I have met through this study who have chosen to resist the path of purely personal gratification and instant pleasure.

Choosing Islam in America is not an easy path. Muslims are considered to be strange by most Americans. Wearing a scarf, refusing social drinks, not gambling, not being patriotic to the United States or Canada—those are not ways to win friends. Some seem to dismiss those who convert as just "not very smart." A study of Muslims in this country would no doubt reveal a very high number of professionals—doctors, engineers, nurses, professors, business men and women, teachers—along with blue collar workers, students, and homemakers.

The prevailing view by many Americans is that Muslims are terrorists, and they are quickly blamed whenever there is an act of terrorism. This prejudice has resulted in many attacks on Muslims. Following the bombing in Oklahoma City, in April 1995, Muslims across the country suffered personal indignities as the media quickly blamed the attack on Muslim terrorists. Many Muslims were spit on, crudely addressed, threatened, or in other ways put down as if they were responsible for the bombing just by being Muslim. Such behavior may not represent the bulk of the American population; however, it does demonstrate a certain bias against a religious minority in this country.

The United States of America was founded by those seeking the opportunity to worship freely and according to their own desires. We who are citizens of the United States have been quite proud of our history of religious freedom. Whether or not we intend to allow that freedom to be equally shared will be tested as Islam and other Eastern religions begin to grow and take their place in this culture. Islam is one of the fastest growing religions on the North American continent, and it is important to know and understand these people who seek to live and find happiness among us.

Sometimes loved ones make choices that cause reactions in us ranging from heart–wrenching to heart–warming. Some choices may push us too far, and we may respond as Tevya did, in *Fiddler On the Roof*, at the marriage of his third daughter when he indicated that there was no "other hand" because if he bent that much (to accept what she had done, who she had married), he would break. By contrast, some choices our daughters make (and sons, too), may open us up to the world around us if we allow ourselves to explore this new path in the spirit of adventure and discovery. Jodi's decision to follow Islam was the beginning of such a walk for my husband and me.

In our walk, we have discovered many wonderful people trying to live full and abundant lives by trying to eliminate the mediocrity of the present–day culture and attempting to bring up their children to respect God and the rights of others. The choice was there to accept or reject, and thanks be to God, we decided to take the road of acceptance. It has been an exciting and fulfilling journey sharing with and learning from these daughters of another path.

❖ ❖ ❖

Appendix A: Letter and Questionnaire:
American-Born Women Converted to Islam
(Collected from September 1993 through July 1994)

TO: American-born women who have converted to Islam
FROM: Carol Anway, a parent whose daughter, Jodi, converted
                    to Islam and Jodi Tahireh Mohammadzadeh, the daugh-
                    ter who converted
RE: A research project to foster understanding of the choice
                    to convert to Islam and the effect of that choice on one's
                    life
DATE: September 1993

Twelve years ago our daughter, Jodi, married a young man from Iran and about two years later converted to Islam. Although we were very accepting of our new son-in-law, it was a struggle to accept this change of religion which Jodi chose. We are so grateful that they lived close enough so that we had time to work through our relationship with her and Reza regarding their lifestyle and traditions that were so new to us. That relationship has been enriched even more by the coming of two grandchildren.

Friends and acquaintances are familiar with the book and movie, *Not Without My Daughter*, and other articles that are very negative. They do not understand the strength and quality of life Jodi and her other American Muslim sisters have in their Islamic commitment. We want to share a more realistic image by gathering and sharing some of your stories through a descriptive research and possible articles or book.

Carol, the director of the research project, has a master's degree in education/counseling. Jodi is working on her master's degree in nursing. We will be assisted by a small group of American-born women who have converted to Islam and are professional educators.

This is a cross-sectional study of women in major urban areas of the United States and Canada. The study is based on those American-born women who have converted to Islam and wear the covering (hijab) whether married or unmarried. Our intent is to gather stories of women from a wide geographical area of the United States and Canada by their completing this questionnaire.

The purpose of this study is to explore and describe the effect that conversion to Islam has had on the lives of American-born women and their families. We want to emphasize the positive aspects as well as acknowledge stresses that have occurred. We hope, through the writings that will result from this study, to encourage the families of origin of American Muslim women to work through their struggle to understand and accept this choice to convert to Islam.

The data in the attached questionnaire contains both objective and subjective questions to answer. This will assist you in describing your experiences as a Muslim woman.

The questionnaire collection period has been extended from May 15 to June 15 but we would like for you to send your completed questionnaire to us as soon as possible.

We want to reinforce the confidentiality of this project. Carol will be the only one who will know what name goes with what data and will be very careful to keep what you share separate from your name. However the data gathered will be used in articles and possibly a book to reflect the data and stories collected.

If you have any questions about the study, please call Carol at 816/252-7541 in the Kansas City area.

Sincerely,

Carol Anway and Jodi Tahireh Mohammadzadeh
P.O. Box 27
Lee's Summit, MO 64063

AMERICAN-BORN WOMEN CONVERTED TO ISLAM
QUESTIONNAIRE
by
Carol Anderson Anway
and
Jodi Tahireh Mohammadzadeh

Directions: Thank you for your willingness to respond to this questionnaire. There are two parts to it. The first and last pages are easy—just collecting information. The rest of the pages present questions for you to respond by writing down your own experiences.

After filling out page one, respond about your own personal experiences using the questions in small print to guide your responses where appropriate. You may write in the spaces on the questionnaire or on separate sheets of paper.

Please feel free to make copies of this questionnaire and introductory letter to give to other American-born women who have converted to Islam. Encourage them to fill it out and return it within 6 weeks after receiving the questionnaire.

I.   STATISTICAL DATA

Age_____   Vocation_____   Work Status_____

Education (Circle highest achieved) Grade School   High School   AA
    BA/BS   MA/MS   Doctorate   Other_____

Education at time of conversion: _____

Marital Status ___Never Married ___Married ___Divorced
___Widowed
If married, nationality of husband_____   Years Married_____

Number of children _____   Ages_____
If school age, are they in   ___Islamic   ___public school   ___home school

How many years have you been Muslim?_____

Check the areas of Islam which you practice:
        ___wear cover (hijab)
        ___daily prayers
        ___fasting during Ramadan
        ___eat only approved meats
        ___on-going study of *Qur'an* and Islamic teachings

Name_____
Phone (_____)_____
Address _____

II.   YOUR CONVERSION TO ISLAM
Describe the process of your conversion to Islam.
What was your religious commitment prior to converting to Islam and
the extent of that commitment?

Describe the changes that you needed to make in your life as a result of
your conversion and practice of Islam. Were there areas left behind that
caused you grief and loss? How has this change helped you be what
you wanted to be? What has been (or is) the most meaningful part of
Islam for you?

III.   LEARNING TO LIVE AND PRACTICE AS A MUSLIM
How did you learn to live as a Muslim?
Who was most helpful to you?
What was most helpful to you?
To what extent has it been easy or difficult for you to take on the
religious practices?

IV.   YOUR FAMILY OF ORIGIN
What effect has your choice to be Muslim had on your relationship
with your parents and other family members?
What do you hope for in regard to your relationship with parents or
family?
What were or are the main points or events of stress (if any) with your
family of origin?

How do you manage the celebration of traditional holiday times?
How do you include your family of origin in your Islamic celebrations?
What are the difficulties or pleasures for you when you visit your family or leave your children with them?

V. YOUR HUSBAND

How did you meet your husband?
What were the characteristics that attracted you to him?
What needs did you have in your life that this man seemed to fill for you?
What part did he have in your conversion?
How did your family of origin accept your husband?
   1. before marriage as your friend
   2. as your fiancee
   3. as your husband
Tell about your marriage ceremony.
What elements of Islam were in the ceremony?

VI. THE HOMELAND OF ORIGIN OF YOUR HUSBAND

To what extent does your daily life include the traditions and culture of your husband's country?
What are your goals in regard to living in your husband's country or U.S./Canada?
What citizenship does your husband now hold?

VII. YOUR HUSBAND'S FAMILY

Have you met your husband's immediate family? If so, tell about the experience.
How have you been accepted by his family?
If you move to the area where his family is, how do you expect to fit in?
What benefits or problems do you anticipate in relating to your husband's family?

VIII. YOUR POSITION AS A WOMAN

What are the rights you are experiencing as a Muslim woman?
What are some areas you are grateful for or are apprehensive about in your position as a woman in your marriage?

What are some areas you feel are not open to you in your position as a Muslim woman?

IX.   CHILD REARING   (If you have children)
How are your child rearing techniques influenced by being Muslim?
To what extent is your husband involved in child care?.
What are your rights and obligations with the children?
What are their rights and obligations to you?

X.   YOUR CHANCE TO EXPRESS OTHER VIEWS AND THOUGHTS
What would you like the American public to know about you that has not yet been asked?

Appendix B:
Questionnaire: Parents of American-Born Women Converted to Islam

(Questionnaires for the parents were sent to most of the women when they responded to the original questionnaire. It was their choice whether or not to send this one on to the parents. A letter was enclosed with the parent questionnaire that was similar to the letter sent with the questionnaire to the women.)

PARENT QUESTIONNAIRE

I. STATISTICAL DATA

Name:

Phone:

Address:

Daughter's Name:

Years Muslim:

Level Ed.:

Level Ed. of Spouse:

Vocation:

Spouse's Vocation:

No. of Children You Have:

On a scale of 1 to 10 rate how you felt about your daughter's conversion to Islam in the first few days you received the news. May indicate both mom and dad.

Rate how you presently feel about your daughter's conversion

1. Tell about your daughter's conversion to Islam.

2. Tell about the effect your daughter's conversion and commitment to Islam has had on the family.

3. What do you hope for in regard to your relationship with your daughter in the future?

4. What were or are the main points or event of stress with your daughter (and husband and grandchildren if applicable)?

5. How do you manage the celebration of traditional holiday times?

6. How are you included in their Islamic celebration or how do you wish to be included?

7. What are the difficulties or pleasure for you when your daughter (and her family, if any) visits in your home or you visit with them?

8. If your daughter is married to a Muslim, tell about the experience of that event for you.

9. At the present time, what are your greatest concerns regarding your daughter and her conversion?

10. What effect, if any, has this experience had on your theology and religious commitment?

Appendix C:
One Women's Story
In Response to the Questionnaire

With many of the responses to the questionnaire came personal notes from the women scribbled in the margin regarding their appreciation of the opportunity to share their story or wanting to know about the responses of others. The following response is written in full to give a sample of one story in total. She expressed in a note that "writing this was an interesting experience—opening up the flood gates would be a good analogy!"

The woman is 35 years old, has three children, works part–time, has a bachelor's degree, and has been Muslim 14 years.

Tell of Your Conversion to Islam

My conversion to Islam was a very long and gradual process. I was raised in a culturally Christian household, a place where the major holidays were celebrated but the deeper meanings left unexplored. This was intentional on the part of my parents who felt that much hatred had been done to the world in the name of organized religion. At the insistence of both sets of grandparents, we children were baptized and given some rudimentary Sunday school training. My parents told us that when we were grown we could pick our own religions, if indeed, we wanted a religion.

My religious training left me with a belief in God (how else could one explain all the wondrous interconnections and intricacies of earth and universe?) but no belief in any system of religion. I considered myself a Christian, but in a broad sense: belief in God, belief in Jesus as a prophet, belief in the moral and ethical teachings. However, my upbringing engendered a high degree of skepticism and cynicism, and I questioned every aspect of church dogma. In the end, I decided that I didn't believe in organized religion as it was illogical, internally inconsistent, and hypocritical (having sanctioned many unethical and immoral acts in the name of God).

However, I had a vague, almost unrecognized idea that without religion something essential was missing from life. A life lived without some sense of a higher purpose was just an empty, random chase after perpetually changing desires. So I began a rather half–hearted, disorganized search for my "spiritual" self.

I saw glimpses of the spiritualism that I was looking for in various religions but they all seemed to be missing some essential ingredient. This one had a beautiful sense of peace and tolerance, but had lost its moral and ethical sense in the meantime. That one had a strong element of personal responsibility to others and a high code of personal conduct, but was repressive and suppressed logical inquiry. Another had a strong sense of religious collectiveness and historical context but promoted exclusivism. Still another understood the mystery, beauty, and peace that surrounds God, but was impractical about everyday matters and forgetful of our responsibilities to our fellow human beings. At about this time, I met the man who later became my husband and in trying to understand him and his culture, I came across Islam. Islam's ideas and teachings appealed to me immediately. They were coherent, they were logical, they were moderate, and they promoted a balance of personal responsibility and collective action. They were inclusive and yet outreaching; God was powerful and yet just; God was merciful and yet exacting. I took my shahada the day my husband and I were married.

My conversion to Islam at first seemed to require no change in my life. My husband, having lived in the U.S. for some years, and I, having been raised here, followed the cultural norm and separated our "religious life" from our "secular life." The first changes (noticeable to those around us) occurred as we began to raise a family and began to make decisions that affected our child and our life together. If there was one definable turning point in our commitment to God, it came when our oldest child was just three years old. I had a good friend who was a practicing Muslim and with whom I spent a great deal of time. My son was a keen observer and quite articulate for his age. One day around Christmas, he questioned why it was that we called ourselves Muslims if we didn't do any of the (observable) things that Muslims do? He wanted to know why we had a Christmas tree. He wanted to know why I didn't wear a scarf.

I didn't have very good answers for him, and his questions prompted a complete evaluation of the role of religion in our lives. My husband and I debated the merits of raising children with or without a strong religious identity and examined how important we felt religion was for ourselves.

In the end, we felt that a sense of religion was important for our child(ren) and, therefore, it was necessary for ourselves as well.

Over the next five years or so we adjusted ourselves and our lifestyle to be within Islamic parameters. Gradually we began to eat only halal foods and avoided social situations that involved alcohol consumption by others. We began to fast Ramadan, to pray all of our prayers, to study the Qur'an, and became more involved in the Muslim community. Generally, becoming more conscious of Islam meant constantly re-evaluating ourselves and our surroundings. At times the constant evaluation felt constrictive, and we longed for the carefree days of the past where life was lived unthinkingly. However, these times were few, and we would never have seriously considered giving up all that we had gained by living Islam.

Living as a practicing Muslim has brought a sense of purpose to my life. There is a pervasive sense of serenity in the knowledge that life is lived for a purpose. I feel that I have become a much better human being—more compassionate, more moderate, more deep-thinking. There is a richness and a calmness in my life that was not there prior to becoming a practicing Muslim. Life in its broadest sense has become one beautiful, intricate whole.

How I Learned to Live and Practice as a Muslim

I learned to live as a Muslim primarily by reading the Qur'an and by asking questions of knowledgeable Muslims. I also watched and observed Muslims around me.

I learned how to pray by reading a book designed to guide new Muslims through the prayer. Any other questions I had, I asked other Muslims. I also drew upon sources and people in my husband's family. My mother-in-law and father-in-law were particularly helpful as were other relatives abroad who sent books or other resources as I needed them.

The ease or difficulty of taking on any specific Islamic practice has always been directly correlated to how I understood it in connection with what I already knew about Islam. If I didn't understand its significance or see its connection to the intricate "whole" of Islam, I found it difficult to integrate into my life. When I had read enough, asked enough questions, talked enough, and finally understood, I didn't have a problem adding that practice into my life.

My Family of Origin

My becoming a *practicing* Muslim has had a very profound effect upon my relationship with my parents. My parents regard Islam quite negatively and consider it an oppressive, dogmatic religion. They don't hold religion, in general, in very high esteem and regard Islam, in particular, to be very oppressive of women. However, my only sibling, my sister, is quite supportive of my choice.

I hope that in the future I might be able to sit and talk with my parents about Islam and its role in my life. We have attempted to discuss it many times but have made very little progress. They seem unable to understand that being Muslim brings me peace and joy and has added immeasurable depth to my life. Islam has not taken anything away from who I am, but has only added to it. My parents seem to regard my choice only as a rejection of them and a rejection of my heritage. They believe that I have committed a form of cultural apostasy and blame themselves. They believe that they failed me—failed to give me strong self–esteem and failed to involve me fully in my own culture. I hope that one day they will accept my choice—perhaps not understand it, but accept it.

There are many points of stress between myself and my parents regarding Islam. They dislike anything that physically marks me (or my children) as "different" (read "Muslim"). They are uncomfortable going out in public with me or my daughters because we wear hijab (myself) or modest clothing (my daughters wear pants under their dresses). They were upset when we asked them to stop drinking alcohol in our house when they visited us. They used to bring it with them. They try not to take a picture of me if I have on my scarf. They don't like our children's Muslim names and argued greatly with me about it when our first child was born. My parents are uncomfortable with my husband's and my insistence that family comes first—they feel that I have sold myself short by staying home (although I do work part–time!) and being family–oriented. They wished a "career" for me. They are uncomfortable with our world outlook and find it to be impractical and idealistic. Except for the fact that they believe we are too conservative, they think we are too politically correct. Frankly, most of the time, I am not sure exactly what they think about me because they never *discuss* it openly. I do know from the uncomfortable, explosive, and divisive conversations we have had, that they disapprove of and are disappointed with my choices in life. They can't, however, ever seem to tell me WHY. I believe it is because they are unable to argue against something that is ethical, moral, moderate, and logical—and is something that they taught me to believe in since I was a small child (only they didn't call it "Islam").

In our holiday celebrations, we attempted with our first-born to continue celebrating Christmas with my parents. We changed the emphasis to "helping Grandma and Grandpa celebrate their holiday" and also spoke about the importance of Prophet Jesus (pbuh) in Islam. It didn't work for many different reasons. Our child was too young to really be able to make that distinction, and peer pressure to be like all the other Christmas celebrants pushed him toward the popular idea of Christmas. My parents used Christmas to push American culture at him creating an "us versus them" environment and creating confusion and tension in our child. As our next children were born we realized that we didn't want these same scenes replicated with them, and so we gradually stopped going to my parents' house for Christmas. It was a decision that both disappointed and angered my parents. They now celebrate Christmas with my sister and her children and husband.

We do send Christmas cards to my parents, my sister, and my surviving grandparent, wish them a Happy New Year, and call them on Christmas Day. We also send my family letters or cards on Eid al-Fitr after Ramadan. My family sends us cards at Christmas and my sister also calls several times during Ramadan to see how we are doing. The other Christian holidays (e.g. Easter) were not celebrated in my family as I was growing up and are not a factor now. My mom sends all the grandchildren cards at Halloween (which we do not celebrate but overlook in deference to my parents), Valentine's Day, and on their birthdays.

We would love to include my parents in our Islamic celebrations, but they are not comfortable with the idea. They will not accompany us to any gatherings with our Muslim friends if they happen to be visiting us, and in deference to my parents, we usually stay home unless it is impossible to get out of the activity.

We have many difficulties when we visit my parents, most springing from their disapproval of our lifestyle. Our world views are quite different—from politics to the role of "independence" and "materialism" in a person's life. We do have many good times with my parents and want a close and mutually respectful relationship with them.

My Husband

I met my husband while I was in college, through mutual friends. The characteristics which most attracted me were his generosity of spirit, honesty, compassion, loyalty, intelligence, and his general strength of character. He knew who and what he was and yet he was humble. I greatly admired his strength of character and his generosity to others. He was very accepting and gentle and yet there was strength inside.

My husband had a large role in my conversion to Islam because he was able to answer all my questions, and he spent a great deal of time explaining both Islam and his culture to me. He always included me in all his Islamic or cultural activities and acted as my interpreter, linguistically and culturally. He made Islam available for me and helped me to experience it firsthand. He never, at any point, pressured me to convert. The decision was entirely mine.

My family didn't accept him very well as my "friend" but were fine after we became "engaged." They like him immensely as a human being but blame him for brainwashing me into becoming Muslim. They also blame me for being so gullible. Our relationship with my parents was very good until we became practicing Muslims. We were married in a civil ceremony at the county courthouse and by proxy in Iran (so that relatives who were "clergy" could perform the ceremony for us). Our civil ceremony contained no Islamic elements and our Islamic ceremony was very basic: the marriage contract, the intent (declaration of desire) to be married, the public announcement of our marriage.

The Homeland of My Husband

We try to run our household on an Islamic model and to the extent that Iranian culture is basically an Islamic culture, our household reflects it. We speak Farsi at home and eat mostly Iranian food although tacos, spaghetti, and stir–fry are big favorites (along with roasts and hamburgers). We intend to live in the U.S. for the forseeable future due to the economic situation in Iran and because we have student loans to repay in this country. We feel that we cannot forsake our debts here, and we could never afford to both live and pay off our loans if we lived in Iran. We have considered moving to another Middle Eastern country. My husband is an Iranian citizen.

My Husband's Family

I have met all the members of my husband's immediate family and some members of the (immense) extended family. I met my mother-in-law and father-in-law before we married, when they visited the United States for a summer. They accepted me very well, although it must have been difficult for them since they are very traditional Muslims and I was your typical twenty-year-old college co-ed. I have been accepted wonderfully by my in-laws although they have disagreed with the way we have done many things, e.g., getting married as undergrads and having three children while my husband was still in graduate school. However, they have never belabored their concerns. My in-laws lived with us for about a year and then moved down the block for the next year after that. It was a great experience, although it had both its ups and downs! I expect that should we move to Iran, I would fit in fairly well and that I would be graciously accepted by the extended family. I might have a few problems with Iranian culture particularly in those areas which deviate from Islamic norms. Any problems from the extended family might arise from my independence and self-reliance.

I have learned a great deal from my in-laws. They have a wonderful way of relating to their children, a way which engenders respect for others and great amounts of self-esteem. It is interesting to see how a child-oriented and religious-oriented culture operates. My in-laws, by virtue of being a contrast to American culture, have given me a great appreciation for certain elements of my American cultural identity. From all my comparing and contrasting of Iranian and American cultures, I have seen that Islam is truly correct in saying that moderation in all is the right path!

My Position as a Woman

As a Muslim woman I experience the full benefits given to me by God as a member of the human race. I am responsible only to God for how I live my life, and how well I fulfill my duties to Him. The most important right which I enjoy by benefit of being a Muslim woman is the right of equality before God. Among the other rights which are detailed for women in Islam are the right to earn and keep our own money, to retain and/or dispose of our own property, the right to inherit, the right to initiate and contest a divorce, the right to an education, the right to retain our own name after marriage, the right to participate in choosing our own mates, the right to custody of our children.

However, as Islam is a just and fair religion, along with my rights come my obligations. All levels of Islamic society—including the individual and on through the relationships of husband/wife, parent/child, employer/employee, and the society/societal member—are firmly connected by interlocking and mutually reciprocal rights and duties. A right does not exist without a corresponding duty; a duty does not exist without a corresponding right. As an example: it is one of my rights as a wife to be financially supported by my husband—that is his obligation. Among others, my obligation is to try and live within his financial means without complaint, derision, or greed, and to care for his property and assets in his absence. My husband is obligated to treat me with courtesy and respect, and I am obliged to do the same for him. As a member of a society, I am obliged to help my fellow members, and they and the societal bureaucracy at large are obligated to help me in my times of need. There is much misunderstanding on the part of non–Muslims (and some Muslims) regarding the absolute inter–connectedness of rights and obligations—they come as a unit and cannot be separated out to be viewed separately without losing their essential qualities.

I feel no apprehension about my position as a Muslim woman in my marriage. I do not feel that there are any areas of private or public endeavor that are closed to me. I do have concerns regarding the status of some women in those societies and within those marriages where there is ignorance of or misunderstanding of the teachings of Islam. There exist many Muslim societies where deviations from the Islamic norms regarding the status and role of women (as well as other issues) have resulted in a constriction of the role of women. "Cultural Islam" very often is at variance with Islam. Verses from the Qur'an and Hadis of the Prophet (pbuh) are often taken out of their context of revelation or transmission and used to support patriarchal cultural viewpoints. Both men and women are often uneducated as to the true meanings of Islamic injunctions and, by default, follow the standard cultural practice of their societies.

Child Rearing

My child–rearing techniques are directly influenced by being a Muslim. Islam touches all parts of my life and as such I try to raise my children in the most Islamic way possible. My children came into this world as Muslims, innocent and submissive to the will of Allah. It is our great responsibility, indeed both a trust and a test from Allah, that my husband and I raise them to remain Muslim.

The most easily observable Islamic influences on our child–rearing techniques include encouraging the children to follow us in prayer, teaching them Qur'anic verses, using traditional Muslim greetings and everyday phrases, encouraging them to dress modestly and behave with compassion and kindness. We use a lot of modeling and verbal encouragement and reminding, but the children are never forced to join us in any given activity as Islam teaches that there is no compulsion in religion. We do, if necessary, insist that the children remain near our activity (while quietly occupying themselves) so that at least they have exposure to the activity and understand that there are some minimal family standards that they must adhere to. We try to be tactful and discreet when enforcing these standards to avoid provoking outright rebellion.

The major way in which Islam influences my child–rearing techniques is that I try to remember that I am always within Allah's sight. Allah has set high standards of personal behavior for humans, not because He is vengeful, but because He knows that we are capable of rising to meet those standards. I am also always aware that my two recording angels are ever watchful! I try to be patient (this one can be quite difficult!), polite, and respectful; and to act with compassion, sincerity, and understanding towards them [the children]. I encourage them to value education and view learning as a life–long endeavor that is not limited to school hours or "school topics." We put great emphasis on doing their personal best at school and elsewhere; to be helpful and kind; not to lie or cheat; to value Allah (and therefore Islam), their family, and their fellow human beings; to stand up for what they believe in, to combine personal piety with outward action; to be sincere and straightforward; and to be generous in thought as well as in action. We also try to view each child as an individual, to view them outside of the influence of birth order, to try not to compare them to their siblings or to ourselves, to try to accept and value those personality traits that are irritating to us but part and parcel of who they are.

Insha'Allah, our children will grow to be compassionate, productive Muslims. To that end we are always re–evaluating our progress and our child–rearing techniques. We always try to follow the specific Islamic injunctions, but also attempt to follow the "spirit of the law."

My husband is very involved with the care of the children. I work part–time, and while I am at work he is their sole caretaker. He also is with the children when I go to meetings or study groups. He takes the kids to the doctors, takes them out on excursions, takes them on errands, goes to the swimming pool with them, and any number of other activities.

My rights and obligations with my children? When people mention Islam/mothers/mother's rights, they are usually referring to child custody in the event of a divorce. Both my husband and I are of the opinion that the children should go with whichever parent is better able to care for them. Of course, in Islam, divorce is allowed, but exhaustive efforts to keep the family unit intact should be made first. In most cases, it is the mother who is better emotionally equipped to raise the children. Unless circumstances warrant differently, the non–custodial parent has the right to frequent visitation. The custodial parent should be helped financially to raise the children, if it is necessary. All divorces should take place in an Islamic family court with a qualified jurist making the decision.

My obligation to my children is to love them, respect them, and help them grow to be Muslim adults. This is as much an obligation to my children as it is to Allah, who placed these children in my care as a trust from Him. I am obliged to remember that my children belong to Allah, not to me—and I must treat them accordingly.

As specified in the Qur'an, my children's obligations to me are that they should respect me (but I must be worthy of that respect), obey me (as long as I am within the bounds of Islam in my request), and care for me if I attain old age. They have the right to expect love, good physical care, and guidance from me. They have the right to be treated with dignity and respect, as I do.

What I Would Like to Express to Others

I would like the American public to know that I am a Muslim by personal choice. I am a fully mature, intelligent human being, capable of making rational decisions. My decision to embrace Islam is not an effort to fit into my husband's culture or family; it is not the result of too little self–esteem; it is not the result of pressure from my husband. I would also like people to understand that Islam is not repressive of women, it does not condone terrorism, and that it is squarely within the Judeo–Christian tradition. I would like people to realize that Islam stands for moderation and modesty and that there are often great discrepancies between the practices of "cultural Islam" and the directives of Islam.

❖ ❖ ❖

Glossary of Islamic Terms

Adhan	The call to prayer.
Alhamdulillah	A phrase often used in conversation meaning "Praise be to Allah."
Allah	Literally "The God." There is no plural, masculine or feminine form of this word in Arabic. This denotes one God who is neither male nor female.
Assalamu alaikum	A common greeting among Muslims meaning "Peace Be Upon You."
Ayah	A verse from the Holy *Qur'an*.
Dawah	Muslim witnessing to non-Muslims.
Deen	Religious obligation or way of life.
Eid	Celebrations/holidays of which there are two main ones. The Eid of Fast-breaking (Eid al-Fitr) comes at the end of the month of Ramadan. The Eid of Sacrifice (Eid al-Adha) remembers the covenant made by God with Prophet Abraham because of Abraham's willingness to sacrifice his son.
Dua	Supplication prayers, individual or learned.
Fiqh	Jurisprudence; science of Islamic law.

Hadith	The second legal source of Islam. Reports of the sayings, deeds, and practices of the Prophet Muhammad. Plural: hadis.
Hajj	The pilgrimage to Mecca one or more times in one's life. One of the Five Pillars of Islam.
Halal	Allowed in Islam.
Haram	Forbidden in Islam.
Hijab	The manner of dress for Muslim women which involves wearing loose, modest clothing and covering the hair.
Imam	A prayer leader or primary religious community scholar.
Insha'Allah	A phrase often used in conversation meaning "If Allah wills."
Islam	The name of the religion.
Koran	An alternate English spelling for *Qur'an*.
Mahar	Dowry at time of marriage.
Mecca	The Muslim holy city in Saudi Arabia; Muslims are to pray facing Mecca; it is the destination of the Muslim pilgrimage.
Mosque (Masjid)	Muslim house of worship.
Muhammad	The last prophet chosen by God and who delivered the message of Islam.
Muslim	A follower of Islam.
Muslima	Muslim woman.
Namaz	Ritual prayers; also called salat.

Nikkah	Islamic marriage contract.
(pbuh)	Initials for the blessing said after saying the name of a revered prophet or holy leader—means Peace Be Upon Him.
Qur'an	The holy book of Islam; the exact words of God (revelation); the ultimate legal source of Islam. Koran is an alternate English spelling for *Qur'an*.
Ramadan	The ninth month of the Muslim lunar year in which Muslims are required to fast for thirty days.
Salat	The five daily obligatory prayers required of Muslims to be performed at specific times facing a specific direction. One of the Five Pillars of Islam.
Shahada	The Creed of Islam, the verbal commitment to become Muslim by stating: "There is no God but Allah, and Muhammad is the Messenger of God."
Shaikh	A religious leader.
Shari'ah	The code of life or law which regulates all aspects of Muslim life.
Shi'a	One of the two major divisions of Islam. The adherents are often called Shiites. (See Sunni.)
Siyam	Fasting during the entire month of Ramadan. Includes total abstinence from food, liquids, and intimate sexual activity from dawn to sunset. One of the Five Pillars of Islam.
Sufi	The mystics; and sufism is the mystical spirituality of Islam.

Sunnah	The Prophet Muhammad's examples, his sayings and deeds.
Sunni	The two major divisions of Islam are Sunni and Shi'a. Ninety-five percent of Muslims are Sunnis. Within these two groups are a number of subgroups or sects.
(SWT)	Initials of Arabic words of remembrance and worship said after saying Allah— means glorious and sublime. Arabic: subbaanahu wa ta'aala.
Tafseer	The study of the meaning of the *Qur'an*; Qur'anic commentaries.
Tawhid	Monotheism—only one God (Allah); no son or partners. Also, all encompassing unity in one's world view.
Ummah	The community or communities of Muslims.
Wajeb	Obligatory actions.
Wali	A male representative involved in arranging the Muslim marriage contract acting for the bride. Means "protector."
Wudu	Cleansing or ablution prior to salat (prayers).
Zakat	The annual tithe payment or purifying tax given to be distributed among the poor or other rightful beneficiaries. One of the Five Pillars of Islam.

Bibliography
Reference Materials for Understanding Islam

Since many of the resources suggested here are not readily available in the local bookstore, information about where to get the books, videos, and tapes has been included as well as cost at the time of the publication of this book.

BOOKS

Abdalati, Hammudah. *Islam in Focus*. Indianapolis: American Trust Publications, 1975.
> Introductory book giving basic concepts of Islam, ideology, and application of Islam to daily life. Recommended by several of the women respondents featured in *Daughters of Another Path*. IQRA' Book Center, 2701 W. Devon Ave., Chicago, IL 60659. Phone 800/521-4272. $5.00.

Ahmad, Khurshid, ed. *Islam: Its Meaning and* Message. Ann Arbor, MI: New Era Publications, 1976.
> Contains fourteen essays by well-known Muslims discussing the basic tenets of Islam designed to give the Western reader a look at Islam the way Muslims see it. IQRA' Book Center, 2701 W. Devon Ave., Chicago, IL 60659. Phone 800/521-4272. $12.00.

Ahsan, Manazir. *Islam: Faith and Practice*. Ann Arbor, MI: New Era Publications, 1980.
> Overview of the faith and practice of Islam. Islamic Book Center, 103-43 Lefferts Blvd, 2nd Fl., Richmond Hill, NY 11419. Phone 718/848-8942. $3.50.

al-Harariyy, Abdullah. *The Summary Ensuring the Personal Obligatory Knowledge of the Religion.*
> Covers the matters that are obligatory for every pubescent Muslim to know about including essentials of belief, prayers, zakat, fasting, hajj, marriage contracts, and dealings. AICP, 4431 Walnut St., Philadelphia, PA 19104. $5.00.

Al-Tantavi, Allama Ali. *A General Introduction to Islam.* Pakistan: Islamic Book Publishers.
> Introduces Islam to those who may be unfamiliar with the religion and practices. Islamic School of Kansas City, 10515 Grandview Road, Kansas City, MO 64137. $10.00.

Armstrong, Karen. *The History of God: The 4000-Year Quest of Judaism, Christianity and Islam.* New York: Alfred A. Knopf, 1993.
> Explores the ways in which the idea and experience of God evolved among the monotheists—Jews, Christians, and Muslims. Available through bookstores.

Ataur-Rahim, Mohammad. *Jesus, a Prophet of Islam.*
> A history of Christian attempts to establish and defend the doctrine of Trinity. IQRA' Book Center, 2701 W. Devon Ave., Chicago, IL 60659. 800/521-4272. $3.00.

Augsburger, David W. *Pastoral Counseling Across Cultures.* Philadelphia: Westminster Press, 1986.
> A professional book to help counselors and pastors gain insight in working with people who are from other cultures or have intercultural concerns. Available through bookstores.

Brooks, Geraldine. *The Nine Parts of Desire: The Hidden World of Islamic Women.* New York: Anchor Books—Doubleday, 1995.
> Focuses on understanding women who veil. Written by a woman who spent six years in the Middle East living among Muslim women. Available through bookstores.

Bucaille, Maurice. *The Bible, the Qur'an, and Science.* Indianapolis: American Trust Publications, 1979.
An important book on Islamic and Christian studies which analyzes the scriptures in the light of modern scientific knowledge. IQRA' Book Center, 2701 W. Devon Ave., Chicago, IL 60659. Phone 800/521-4272. $9.00.

Esposito, John. *Islam: The Straight Path.* New York: Oxford University Press, 1988.
Introduces the faith, belief, and practice of Islam from its earliest origins up to its contemporary resurgence. KAZI Publication, 3023-27 W. Belmont Ave., Chicago, IL 60618. Phone 312/267-7001. $15.95.

Faruqi, Lamya 'al. *Women, Muslim Society, and Islam.* Indianapolis: American Trust Publications.
A creative educational collection that is particularly helpful for women. American Trust Publications, 10900 W. Washington St., Indianapolis IN 46231, Phone 317/839-9278.

Grob, Leonard, Riffat Hassan, and Gordon Haim, eds. *Women's and Men's Liberation: Testimonies of the Spirit.* New York: Greenwood Press, 1991.
Writings by a number of authors that explore the relationships of equality of men and women. Available through bookstores.

Haddad, Yvonne Yazbeck. *The Muslims of America.* Oxford University Press, 1991.
Covers the history, organization, activism, and intellectual contributions of one of America's fastest growing minorities. IQRA' Book Center, 2701 W. Devon Ave., Chicago, IL 60659. Phone 800/521-4272. $21.00.

Hamid, Abdul Wahid. *Islam: The Natural Way.*
> A book about Islam clearly written and simply presented. Describes Islamic beliefs and reveals the world as viewed by Islam. Excellent for Muslims and non-Muslims. Muslim Educational and Literary Service (MELS), 61 Alexandra Road, Herdon, London NW42RX

Haneef, Suzanne. *What Everyone Should Know about Islam and Muslims.* Chicago: KAZI Publications.
> A thorough explanation of all aspects of Islam written by an American Muslim woman convert for an American audience. KAZI Publication, 3023-27 W. Belmont Ave., Chicago, IL 60618. Phone 312/267-7001. $15.95.

Kolocotronis, Jamilah. *Islamic Jihad: An Historical Perspective.* Indianapolis: American Trust Publications, 1990.
> Doctoral dissertation on the history and meaning of jihad. Islamic School of Kansas City, 10515 Grandview Road, Kansas City, MO 64137. $10.00.

Mawdudi, Sayyid A. *Towards Understanding Islam.* Ann Arbor, MI: New Era Publications, 1980.
> A brief, clear view of Islam, presenting basic beliefs and practices of Islam for the Muslim and non-Muslim audience. IQRA' Book Center, 2701 W. Devon Ave., Chicago, IL 60659. Phone 800/521-4272. $5.00.

Mohammad, Marith Udeen. *Prayer and Al-Islam.* Chicago: Mohammed Islamic Foundation.
> An informative book on the basic tenets of the religion from an African-American perspective. W.D. Muhammad Publications, P.O. Box 1944, Calumet City, IL 60409.

Phillips, Abu Ameenah Bilal. *The True Religion.*
A comprehensive to-the-point book that is based solely on Qur'an and Sunnah. Sums up the message and universality of Islam, the message of false religion, and recognition of Allah. Halalco Bookstore, 108 E. Fairfax St., Falls Church, VA 22046 Phone 703/532-3202.

Poston, Larry. *Islamic Da'wah in the West.* New York: Oxford University Press, 1992.
An exploration of Islamic missionary activity as it has evolved in contemporary Western societies. Available through bookstores.

Qayyum, A. *On Striving To Be A Muslim.*
Shows how one who strives hard can be in spiritual accord with the demands of the Divine Will as learned through the Prophets and finally God's Messenger. KAZI Publication, 3023-27 W. Belmont Ave., Chicago, IL 60618, Phone 312/267-7001. $9.95.

Rahman, Afzalur. *Role of Muslim Women in Society.*
A complete guide on the topic, presenting the role of women according to the *Qur'an* and Sunnah. Presents the Muslim woman as seen through Muslim eyes. IQRA' Book Center, 2701 W. Devon Ave., Chicago, IL 60659. Phone 800/521-4272 $21.00.

Wormser, Richard. *American Islam: Growing Up Muslim in America.* New York: Walker Publishing Co., 1994.
Presents the Muslim American experience based on interviews with American Muslim teenagers. Small, easy-to-read book also gives overview of Islamic history. Available through bookstores. $15.95.

Yusseff, M.A. *The Dead Sea Scrolls, The Gospel of Barnabus, and the New Testament.* Indianapolis: American Trust Publications, 1986.
A history of the Bible from an Islamic perspective. Islamic Book Service, 2622 E. Main St., Plainfield, IN 46168.

VIDEOS

Choosing Islam
> Documentary interviewing Americans—men, women, black and white—who have chosen Islam. Includes some basic information about the faith and why they chose it. Sound Vision, 843 W. Van Buren #411, Chicago, IL 60607. Phone 800/432-4262. $14.95.

Islam, Yusuf (formerly Cat Stevens). *Journey from Singing Stardom to Peace of Soul*
> Islamic Association of North America, P.O. Box 833010, Richardson TX 75083.

Lang, Jeffrey. *Struggling to Surrender: Some Impressions of an American Convert to Islam.*
> A personal account of one man's journey in search for God in the midst of a culture that places minimal value on such a quest. Easy to identify with his experience which is straightforward and touchingly expressed. IBTS, PO Box 5153, New York, NY 11105. Phone 718/721-5381. $14.95.

MAGAZINES

The American Muslim
> Produced quarterly; an open forum for the free expression and discussion of ideas and issues of concern to Muslims in America. The American Muslim, P.O. Box 5670, Bel Ridge, MO 63121. Phone 314/291-3711 (fax). $18.00 per year.

Islamic Horizons
> Produced bi-monthly; offical magazine of the Islamic Society of North America. ISNA, P.O. Box 38, Plainfield, IN 46168. $24 per year in USA; $28 per year in Canada.

Islamic Sisters International
> Produced bi-monthly. A networking magazine for Muslim sisters. ISI, P.O. Box 501 Independence, KS 67301. $20 per year.

The Message
Published montly by the Islamic Circle of North America. ICNA, 166-26 89th Ave., Jamaica NY 11432. Phone 718/658-5163. $28.00 per year.

Minaret
Published monthly by the Islamic Center of Southern California. ICSC, 434 S. Vermont Ave., Los Angeles CA 90020. Phone 213/384-4570. $25 per year.

Sisters!
Coming early in 1996, a glossy full–color magazine of dialogue among Muslim women. Available from Amica International, 1201 1st Ave. So., Suite 203, Seattle, WA 98124. Phone 800/622-9256.

PAMPHLETS

Haddad, Yvonne Y. *A Century of Islam in America.*
A brief review of the Muslim movement in America (12 pages). Available from Islamic Affairs Program, The Middle East Institute, Washington, DC 20036.

Islam at a Glance
A brochure giving a brief overview of Islam; other titles available. The Muslim Students' Association of the US and Canada, P.O. Box 38, Plainfield, Indiana 46168. Phone 317/839-8157.

INDEX

ablutions 67, 132

Adam 30, 66, 170

adultery 66

age range 6

alcohol 75, 137, 146, 147,
149, 187, 188

alcoholic 146, 149, 150

Allah 5, 22, 26-28, 31, 33, 37,
38, 41, 57, 62, 65-69, 73,
74, 81, 86, 90, 98,
114, 117, 132, 144,
161-163, 165-167, 169, 193, 194

America . . . . . . iv, vi, 3, 4, 6, 27, 32,
75, 78, 91, 111, 113, 128,
139, 161, 164, 168, 170, 171, 174

American-born . v, vii, 2-6, 8, 11, 41,
77-179, 183

Angel Gabriel 5, 65

angels 39, 105, 193

Arabic . . . 31, 64, 65, 67, 68, 70, 84,
105, 122-125, 127, 131, 138, 162

aunt 27, 61

bachelor's degree . . . 6, 25, 111, 185

baptize 17

beliefs . . . 1, 6, 22, 24, 26, 32, 36-39,
41, 42, 54, 55, 59, 65, 72, 79,
81, 83, 108, 132, 145, 154,
156-158, 161, 172

Bible . 12, 15, 30, 40, 41, 58, 82, 171

birthday 99, 151, 152

black 28, 32, 33, 74

blood sacrifice 15, 30

born-again 11, 13

brainwashed 55, 104, 161, 162

brothers 12, 20, 49, 52-54, 73,
120, 133, 148, 151, 155

Canada . . . . viii, 3-5, 77, 86, 112,
114, 123, 177, 178, 181

celebration . . 71, 99, 112, 149, 151,
152, 181, 184

charity 71, 72

cheating 66, 146

children . . . . vi, 4, 7, 11, 21, 22,
24, 28, 46, 48, 54-56, 70, 71, 73, 80,
81, 84, 86, 101, 103, 104, 109,
112-114, 120, 124, 125, 127,
139-144, 146-150, 153-156,
159-164, 168, 170, 171, 175, 179,
181-183, 185, 186, 188, 189,
191-194

Christ 1, 11, 29, 40, 49, 56, 104, 157

Christian . . vi, 5, 9, 11-13, 15-17, 19,
20, 24, 32-34, 37, 40, 50,
51, 54, 56, 66, 79, 88, 97,
113, 121, 123, 129, 149-151,
153, 156, 162-164, 169, 171,
185, 189, 195

Christianity . 4, 29, 30, 35-37, 39, 43,
50, 59, 60, 63, 90, 111, 167

Christmas 50, 72, 90, 106, 141,
149-153, 163, 186, 189

church . . 1, 9, 11, 13-19, 29, 30, 33,
36, 39, 44, 50, 51, 63, 65,
93, 95, 121, 122, 129, 185

church attendance 12-13

cleanliness 134

college 6, 7, 9, 10, 22, 25, 29, 30, 33,
37, 40, 42, 49, 90, 97, 101, 103,
104, 114-116, 120, 190, 191

commitment 2, 5, 6, 11, 13, 16,
17, 49, 52, 56, 69, 71, 82, 92, 102,
112, 113, 131, 132, 140, 149, 177,
180, 184, 186

community 2, 7, 9, 27, 71, 73,
77, 82, 85, 86, 107, 115,
133, 146, 187

concerns 29, 47, 48, 102,
106, 109, 153, 154, 184, 191, 192

confusion . . 14, 25, 27, 36, 109, 189

conversion . iv, v, 17, 22, 23, 25, 26,
32, 34, 35, 48, 50, 51, 54-56, 66, 93,
96-98, 100-103, 108, 116, 128, 160,
173, 178-181, 183-186, 190

course 34, 38, 40, 42, 51, 67,
            69, 72, 115, 117, 123, 128,
            133, 137, 139, 157, 194
cover . . . 3, 5, 23, 43, 49, 58, 63, 70,
            73, 74, 76-78, 123, 130,
            148, 162, 166, 169, 180
covering 3, 68, 73-76, 78,
            79, 81, 101, 148, 172, 177
creation 32
cross 2, 37, 39, 177
cult 57
culture 24, 35, 79, 83, 85, 91,
            100, 126-128, 145, 166, 169, 171,
            174, 175, 181, 186, 188-191, 194
daily prayers . . . 7, 68, 146, 156, 180
daughters . . . . . . 1, 3, iv, vi, vii, 2, 3,
            11, 12, 21, 28, 47, 49, 81, 85, 97,
            134, 146, 159, 160, 173, 175, 188
dawah 79
denomination 14
devil 12, 56, 61
disciplines 67
discrimination 76, 101, 102
diversity 100, 103, 145
divinity 38, 40, 66
divorce 7, 24, 32, 49, 101, 120,
            192, 194
doctorate 6, 179
dowry 85, 122
drinking 12, 25, 188
education 4, 22, 81, 86, 87,
            101, 132, 135, 138, 141, 143,
            168, 177, 179, 192, 193
educational level 6
Eid 71, 106, 149-153, 189
emotional 9, 23, 35, 60
emotions 11, 46
extended family . . . 34, 49, 140, 143,
            154, 191
facts 15, 56, 162
faith 2, 5, 6, 15-17, 21, 29, 30,
            42, 51, 53, 62, 65-67, 75,
            77, 82, 88, 90, 93, 95, 98,
            100, 105, 122, 141, 156, 164, 165
faith journey 17, 42, 82

families 2, 4, 7, 12-14, 42, 44,
            46, 47, 49, 52, 53, 56,
            57, 61, 62, 85, 113, 121,
            123, 139, 41, 146, 147, 149, 150,
            154, 158-160, 165, 178
family . . . . . . v, vi, 2, 5, 9, 11, 15-17,
            20, 21, 24, 26, 29,
            31, 33-35, 38, 43, 46-50,
            52-62, 69, 74, 79, 81,
            82, 87, 90, 91, 93, 95, 96,
            100-108, 112-115, 117-119,
            121, 126, 128, 129, 131, 132,
            134-136, 138, 140,
            141, 143, 145-158, 160, 162,
            164, 166, 168, 173, 180,
            181, 184, 186-191, 193, 194
family of origin 47, 48, 52, 57,
            62, 91, 103, 113, 152,
            153, 158, 180, 181, 188
fasting 7, 22, 67, 68, 71, 72,
            75, 84, 146, 149, 180
fasts 7
father 1, 10, 12-16, 35, 47,
            48, 50, 51, 55, 58, 61, 88,
            94, 98-101, 103, 105, 112,
            115, 121, 123, 124,
            131-133, 148, 150, 153
Five Pillars 42, 66, 68
forbidden 7, 79, 146, 154
forgiveness 30, 108, 132
friends 1, 2, 5, 13-15, 20, 26,
            28, 29, 33-35, 42, 49, 55,
            60, 63, 67, 80, 81, 91, 94,
            96, 99, 106, 109, 114,
            116, 117, 120-122,
            127, 129, 135, 138,
            140, 141, 146, 159,
            174, 177, 189, 190
fundamental 11, 65, 66
fundamentalist 51, 166, 170
gifts 55, 71, 79, 90, 121, 125,
            149-153

God .... v, 1, 2, 5, 9, 11-17, 19, 22,
        23, 26-30, 32, 36, 41, 47, 49,
        54, 59, 60, 63, 65-67, 70,
        72, 82, 86, 90-94,
        96, 99, 105, 122, 129, 131,
        132, 139, 141, 144, 156,
        157, 161, 164, 166-170, 172,
        175, 185, 186, 191
gospel 11
graduate 6, 191
grandchildren ... 102, 131, 155, 159,
        184, 189
grandma 108, 131, 145, 189
grandmother 9, 51, 60, 104
grandpa 189
grandparents ... 49, 55, 61, 154, 155,
        159, 185
green card 120
grief 1, 5, 8, 45, 52, 60, 90,
        108, 109, 112, 180
guilt 33, 39, 40
hadith 4, 34, 70, 84, 142
hajj 31, 72
halal 7, 77, 82, 84,
        88, 91, 135, 146, 147,
        149, 150, 156, 187
haram 135, 146, 147
healing 9, 46, 56, 64, 107, 108,
        159, 160
hell 12, 15, 33, 38, 39, 49, 51,
        54, 59, 60, 81, 100, 105, 109
high school 6, 12, 14, 15, 27,
        33, 35, 37, 141, 179
hijab ... 3, 7, 40, 44, 47, 48, 51, 53,
        58, 67, 74-78, 84, 86, 90, 91,
        100, 127, 130, 139, 148, 154,
        161, 166, 169, 177, 180, 188
holidays .. 55, 61, 84, 99, 102, 149-
        153, 158, 163, 185, 189
Holy Spirit 16

home 4, 7, 9-11, 17, 19,
        20, 23, 28, 31, 33, 35, 49, 50, 52,
        53, 57, 69, 80-82,
        87, 89, 96, 103, 104, 111,
        113, 124, 129, 132, 134,
        135, 137, 140, 141, 143, 144,
        147, 159, 170, 171, 173, 179,
        184, 188-190
home school ... 7, 50, 134, 137, 179
hostage crisis 10
husband ..... v, 1, 7, 11, 17, 20-24,
        27, 28, 31, 34, 36-38, 40-42, 48, 52,
        54-57, 59, 60, 62, 67, 70, 72, 82,
        84, 85, 87-90, 98-101, 104, 109,
        111, 113-121, 123-128, 132-144,
        148, 150, 152, 155, 156, 161-163,
        167, 169, 171, 173, 175, 179, 181,
        182, 184, 186, 189-195
imam 72, 116, 117, 167
immigrants 4, 91
international 29, 76, 92, 101
Islam ...... v, vi-viii, 2-8, 11, 17-19,
        21, 26-29, 32, 41-44, 47- 56,
        58-61, 63-75, 77- 79, 81, 83- 86,
        88-91, 93, 95-98, 100, 104, 108,
        111, 113-119, 122, 123, 128,
        132-136, 141, 146, 153, 158,
        162-171, 173-175, 177- 181,
        183-195
Islamic countries 26, 74
Islamic dress 74, 117
Islamic principles .. vi, 2, 63, 73, 92,
        134, 139, 143
Jesus 10, 11, 15, 16, 19, 28,
        30, 36, 41, 44, 66, 99, 104, 105,
        121, 150, 157, 161, 185, 189
Jesus as God 36
Jews 24, 41, 66, 161,
        166
jihad 64, 64, 91, 92
Judaism 4, 11, 24
Judeo 5
judgment 25, 66, 136
Koran 5, 65

life ...... v, 1, 2, 4, 5, 9, 14, 16, 18,
19, 23, 25-30, 32, 33, 39, 42, 44,
46, 49, 50, 52, 53, 56, 57, 59, 60,
63-67, 69, 73, 78, 83, 84, 86-91,
93, 94, 98-100, 102-105, 107,
108, 111, 112, 114, 117, 119,
122, 127-129, 131, 132, 135,
138, 141, 149, 159, 161,
164-171, 173, 177, 180,
181, 185-189, 191, 193
life after death 65, 66
lifestyle ..... vi, 4, 7, 11, 35, 49, 50,
56, 57, 60, 67, 68, 73, 84, 93, 97,115,
135, 145, 159, 169,
177, 187, 189
loss . 7, 33, 60, 62, 90, 108, 165, 180
lunar 71
lying 66, 146
mahar 88, 117
male 19, 21, 73, 78, 80,
81, 99, 113, 119, 133, 148, 169
marriage   vi, 1, 7, 21-24, 33, 38, 45,
54, 57, 69, 84, 88, 98, 101,
104, 109, 111, 112, 114-124,
155, 168, 175, 181, 190, 192
masjid 31, 86
master's degree 111, 177
matrimonial 116
meat 77, 82, 89, 132,
146, 149, 156
meats 7, 20, 82, 84, 146,
147, 180
Mecca 65, 67, 68, 72
media 5, 7, 55, 56, 64, 113,
120, 148, 173, 174
men 21, 41, 73, 76, 78-80, 86,
88, 98-100, 113, 114, 118-120,
123, 128, 130, 131, 148, 163,
166, 174, 192
menstruating 68
menstruation 71
message 30, 65, 178
messenger 22, 66, 67, 132
minister 12, 15, 17, 35, 54, 121, 122
ministers 11, 37

mom 3, 14, 19, 21, 48, 50-52,
56, 59, 60, 63, 95, 117, 134,
148, 150, 151, 154, 155, 157,
183, 189
money 15, 25, 88, 118, 191
moral 9, 13, 77, 167, 185,
186, 189
moral standards 13
morality 66, 73
morals 49, 80
mosque 7, 69, 101, 115, 116,
122, 151, 168
Mother ... 6, 14, 16, 35, 47, 50, 51,
54-56, 58-61, 69, 81, 89, 94, 97,
98,101, 103, 105-107, 115, 119,
121, 124, 125, 127, 132-133,
139, 140, 142, 150, 153, 155,
159, 165, 194
Muhammad 4, 5, 22, 64-67, 80,
85, 99, 136, 140, 170
murder 66
Muslim . iv-viii, 1-8, 19, 27, 29, 32,
34-36, 38-42, 48-59, 62- 68, 70-89,
91, 93, 97, 98, 100-103, 107, 111,
113-121, 125, 126, 128-136,
138-141, 143, 44, 146-149, 151,
153, 154, 156, 159-170, 173, 174,
177, 178, 180-194
Muslim men 21, 128
Muslim women ... viii, 2, 8, 34, 67,
81, 87, 91, 148, 159, 160, 163,
167- 170, 178, 191
namaz 131
negative 5, 7, 27, 46, 55,
64, 106, 120, 140, 173, 177
nikkah 117, 122
non-Muslim 21, 62
obligation 22, 71, 73, 133, 139,
140, 192, 194
obligatory 67-69, 146, 156
Old Testament 12, 30, 66
oneness of God 65, 66
oppressed 34, 161, 163, 165,
166, 169
original sin 15, 30, 36
overseas 54, 61

parent 97, 108, 132, 177, 183, 192, 194
parents .... vi, vii, 1, 13, 16, 33, 35, 44, 46-47, 49-51, 53, 56, 58, 60, 62, 73, 74, 80, 81, 93-97, 100, 102, 104, 106-109, 112, 119-121, 124, 126, 132, 133, 136-139, 142, 147-150, 152-159, 62, 173, 180, 183, 185, 188-190
pastor 15
pastors 24, 30
path ...... iv, vi, viii, 1, 2, 3, 9, 21, 25, 38, 43, 52, 62, 63, 67, 89, 110, 111, 114, 29, 134, 144, 146, 159, 160, 169, 173- 175, 191
peace ... 23, 25, 36, 37, 40, 53, 54, 65, 68, 72, 0, 121, 122, 153, 160, 161, 166-168, 172, 186, 188
pilgrimage 67, 72, 73
political 4, 86, 157, 161, 167
politics 50, 73, 102, 189
pork 7, 12, 27, 55, 58, 82, 84, 146, 147, 149, 155
positive 6, 7, 46, 69, 102, 106, 119-121, 128, 132, 154, 165, 173, 178
power 7, 31, 109, 123, 153
practice 5, 21, 24-29, 33, 54, 64, 67, 69, 71, 73, 79, 80, 83, 85, 100, 113, 114, 128, 132, 135, 136, 148, 151, 156, 162, 171, 180, 187, 192
prayer ... 25, 28, 48, 64, 67, 69-71, 91, 109, 122, 129, 131, 132, 140, 151, 153, 156, 157, 168, 187, 193
prayers 7, 22, 28, 41, 67, 70, 131, 134, 146, 156, 157, 180, 187
praying 9, 16, 64, 68, 70, 75, 84, 95, 156
prejudice 158, 161, 174
prejudices 77, 79
Principles of Islam 2, 5

prophet . 4, 24, 30, 38, 39, 41, 65-67, 80, 136, 140, 142, 170, 185, 189, 192
prophethood 41, 65
prostrating 69
prove 36, 37, 63, 76, 154
questionnaire ... vii, 5, 6, 21, 62, 67, 97, 103, 114, 119, 128, 141, 158, 170, 177-179, 183, 185
Qur'an 4, 5, 22, 25, 29, 31, 34, 35, 42, 47, 51, 52, 56, 65, 66, 70, 73, 83-86, 114, 122, 127, 133-135, 139, 140, 150, 157, 165, 180, 187, 192, 194
Ramadan 7, 25, 38, 41, 67, 71, 72, 75, 76, 80, 116, 146, 149, 180, 187, 189
readiness 16, 28, 108
reconciliation 56, 96, 106-109
rejected 53, 61, 64
rejection 1, 44, 46, 56, 82, 96, 108, 147, 169, 188
relationships   vi, 33, 44, 46, 49, 52, 57, 62, 91, 93, 96, 119, 120, 130, 145, 148, 149, 158, 192
relatives   vi, 2, 9, 43, 53, 62, 73, 81, 99, 109, 123, 125, 151, 153, 163, 187, 190
religion ... 4, 11-14, 17, 18, 21-23, 25, 28, 33, 34, 38, 39, 47, 48, 50-52, 53-58, 60-65, 69, 74, 81, 83, 90, 93-95, 97-99, 102, 103, 109, 113, 114, 128, 133, 162, 164, 167, 168, 171, 172, 177, 185- 188, 192, 193
religious .... viii, 2, 11, 13, 14, 16-18, 25, 30, 32, 34, 41, 42, 46, 47, 9, 57, 61, 67, 70-72, 74, 75, 80, 85, 90, 94, 95, 99, 101-103, 108, 113, 115, 116, 120, 122, 128, 138, 144, 145, 149, 154, 156, 157, 160, 167, 172, 174, 180, 184-186

respect 34, 57, 59, 86, 87, 100, 102, 106, 112, 114-116, 130, 133, 135-137, 142-144, 150, 152-154, 156, 157, 159, 166, 172, 175, 191, 192, 194

rights ...... iv, 77, 85-87, 91, 140, 142-144, 162, 164, 165, 167-169,171, 175, 181, 182, 191, 192, 194

ritual 69

sacrifice 15, 30, 39

salat 68, 69

Satanic 140

savior 24, 38

scarf ... 3, 20, 45, 47, 54, 67, 74-76, 79, 130, 145, 170, 174, 186, 188

scarves 56

school ... v-7, 12, 14-17, 27, 28, 33, 35, 38, 42, 50, 65, 133, 134, 137, 140-142, 146, 155, 156, 163, 179, 185, 191, 193

schools 7, 12, 70, 138-141, 164

search 32, 97, 107, 186

searching 11, 16, 18, 21, 30, 32, 35, 44

sexual 71

sexuality 99, 168

shaikh 80, 122

sin 15, 30, 36, 39, 52

sins 15, 38, 122, 132, 171

sisters 2, 12, 18, 25, 29, 32, 49, 52, 56, 58, 60, 76, 77, 92, 99, 101, 133, 150, 151, 153, 169, 177

siyam 71

socialize 84

society ... vi, 2-4, 7, 16, 26, 48, 53, 63, 73, 78, 83-86, 89, 115, 129, 140, 162, 167, 168, 171, 192

spiritual ... 9, 15, 16, 32, 44, 69, 71, 72, 80, 86, 90, 108, 129, 164

stability 14, 15, 128

stealing 66

stereotype 118, 170

stereotypical 34

strength 2, 5, 26, 95, 103, 108, 112, 113, 159, 160, 163, 177, 190

stress 46, 48, 51, 57, 74, 82, 99, 152, 158, 180, 184, 188

stresses 100, 145, 178

stressful 46, 56, 82, 125, 147

struggle ... 1, 32, 45, 50, 52, 64, 65, 71, 92, 97, 160, 165, 177, 178

studied 17, 25, 32, 50, 65, 131

study ... 7, 8, 15, 17, 21, 24, 25, 29, 31, 34, 35, 45, 83, 95, 109, 115, 129, 135, 162, 168, 174, 177, 178, 180, 187, 194

submission 65, 140, 144

tafseer 141

tawhid 66

television 140, 148, 154

terrorist 64

tolerance 101, 102, 186

tradition 1-3, 49, 52, 74, 79, 85, 92, 101, 121, 122, 128, 132, 173, 195

Trinity 16, 19, 30, 36, 37, 39

TV 13, 80, 113, 135, 148

ummah 31, 73, 85, 91

unclean 70, 82, 147

Unity of Allah 66

values 9-11, 15, 49, 80, 99, 101, 105, 107, 133, 135, 138, 145, 165, 168, 171

veil 74, 78, 79, 168

veiled 3, 79

virgin birth 24

visit 9, 25, 31, 48, 51, 53,
54, 56, 57, 63,
82, 123, 124, 126, 128, 130,
146, 147, 155,
156, 173, 181,
184, 189
visits 57, 123, 127, 184
wedding . 11, 19, 31, 104, 117, 121,
122, 125
western 2, 4, 5, 77, 80, 86, 91,
107, 121, 138, 149, 169
wife 14, 21, 27, 31, 59, 81, 87,
89, 100, 102, 112, 116, 118,
123, 132, 143, 165, 192
woman . . . v, 21, 28, 33, 40, 74, 77-
82, 85-87, 89, 91, 101,
113, 118, 119, 125, 126,
136, 148, 162, 163,
166, 169, 172,
178, 181, 182,
185, 191, 192
women 3-viii, 2, 3, 5-8, 11-14,
16-19, 21, 22, 24, 26, 28-30,
32, 34, 36, 38, 41, 42, 46, 47,
52, 56, 61, 62, 64, 67, 68, 71, 73-83,
85-87, 89, 91, 97- 99, 109, 113, 114,
116, 119-121, 123, 125, 126, 128,
130-134, 136, 141, 143, 144,
146-150, 158-160, 163, 164,
166-171, 174, 177-179, 183, 185,
188, 191, 192, 195

work 4, 7, 10, 11, 16, 23, 28,
31, 42, 43, 46, 49, 52, 57, 63,
67, 69, 77, 80,
81, 88, 89, 101,
103, 106, 108, 109,
112, 118, 120, 122, 123,
125, 135, 137, 142, 145, 152,
158-160, 162, 163, 168, 169,
172, 177-179, 188, 189, 194
world . . . . v, viii, 1, 4, 5, 11,
13, 18, 20, 21, 27,
33, 35, 50, 64, 65,
73, 87, 91, 93, 94,
102, 140, 145, 149,
156, 158, 160, 161,
167, 170, 175, 185,
188, 189, 193
worship 2, 30, 41, 68, 71, 72,
84, 87, 114, 129,
166, 170, 172,
174
wudu 68, 69, 84
zakat 72

Quotes from Readers of
Daughters of Another Path

From American women converts to Islam:
--You have addressed the topic in such a professional and eloquent way. I appreciate the fairness and objectivity of your commentary.
--I read your book in one evening. I was impressed and enthralled with this book.
--I marvel at the fact that many of the sisters' responses (in the book) could have come from me.
--I have been studying Islam intensely and want you to know your book provides one of the clearest, most concise, objective, and fair accounts I've found yet.

Elderly Christian couple's response: We not only fully agree with this beautiful example of genuine spiritually motivated reconciliation, we thank God you were enabled to produce this great testimony of reconciliation.

From Dr. John Esposito, Director of the Center for Muslim-Christian Understanding:
I believe this book is an important one. It provides the reader with an insight into a little recognized phenomenon, and that is both the presence of Muslims in America but more specifically those women who are embracing Islam in an American context. The combination of biography and analysis reveals why and how they have come to Islam, their diverse backgrounds and the issues that each and all face.

From a Christian Theologian with a Major University--The writing is clear, restrained, capable of inducing strong emotional reactions, especially in the form of the engendering of empathy. One wants to meet many of these women of whom you wrote.

A Muslim monthly newspaper: It breaks all the idols of stereotyping and propaganda about Muslim women--those mysterious, quiet, proud people, all covered up except for their hands and faces. . . *Daughters of Another Path* is must reading for all Muslims and for all non-Muslims who have been confused about Islam by what they see in the media.

American Male Muslim Convert--I finished [your book] the second day I received it. After the Holy Quran, it is one of the best books on Islam I have received. . . . Your book will, Insh'allah, help to build bridges of understanding.